Rick Steves'
European Christmas

by Rick Steves
and Valerie Griffith

Table of Contents

A CHRISTMAS IN EUROPE

EUROPE IS MY FAVORITE PLACE TO TRAVEL, with a charming, diverse mix of peoples and traditions. And Christmas is my favorite holiday. For those who celebrate the birth of Jesus, for people surrounded by a loving family, for children filled with wonder, dreaming of goodies under the tree . . . it's the best day of the year. We hope that, by immersing ourselves in the vivid holiday traditions of Europe in this book, our own Christmas season will have a little more meaning, a little more diversity, and a little more sparkle. Merry Christmas!

The birth of Jesus of Nazareth gave Christians a reason to celebrate in winter.

CHRISTMAS: FACT OR FICTION?

CHRISTMAS IS A SEASON of mystery and magic. For kids, it's a time when adults take their visions of the supernatural seriously. For Christians, it's the first miraculous episode in the life of the Son of God on Earth. For everyone, it's a time to celebrate with loved ones, a joyous respite from the mid-winter blahs.

And for historians? Well, unfortunately for historians, the "magic" of Christmas can be a problem. Scholars debate the accuracy of the Bible's account of Jesus' birth, but any book about the way various cultures celebrate Christmas will be full of fanciful legends. As Napoleon once asked, "What is history but a legend agreed upon?"

An Italian church at dawn on Christmas—soon the bells will ring for joy.

But is Christmas real? For Christians, the birth of Jesus is the cornerstone of their faith: the belief that God gave his son to live on Earth among us to empathize with our mortal experience and share his Father's will with us. The place of Jesus' birth, Bethlehem, was the first stop on the Christmas-to-Easter journey that ultimately led to the Crucifixion, where our salvation was earned.

How literally should we take the Bible's account of that first Christmas? That depends on your brand of religion. Taken literally, it's a historical record of three kings arriving 12 days after a young woman gave birth, and presenting gifts of gold, frankincense, and myrrh to an infant wrapped in swaddling clothes. Taken on faith, it's a rich story that believers can use to understand the greatest gift ever given.

Christmas brings families together and fills children with wonder.

Of course, just as most of Europe's greatest churches sit on the remains of pagan temples, the Christmas story is founded on the remnants of pagan history. These lusty pre-Christian legends enliven traditional Christmas festivals, injecting many of the fun cultural differences that make the holiday season in Europe as varied as travel there is in general.

Whether Christmas is about leading you out of the darkness of winter, out of the darkness of sin, or just out of the cold into a warm home and a kiss under the mistletoe—it is a wondrous event. It's a time to bask in the glow of childhood memories, to remember the importance of loved ones in our lives, and to practice the virtue of kindness even to those who might not necessarily deserve it. For most people—at least in our culture—it's the best holiday of the year.

Historians might object to the legends and myths that tinsel the Christmas story told in this book, but I'm writing from a love of the mystery of Christmas, not for strict historical accuracy, so I won't be bogged down by a scholarly approach to history. If the Bible says it happened, that's good enough for me. If locals tell it to me, it's a part of them and their celebrations, so I pass it along to you. In researching this book, I learned that nobody really knows much of anything for sure about the misty origins and meanings of the many legends associated with Christmas. If you're the type of person who needs everything to be a proven fact . . . you're probably not reading this book.

Now, as you anticipate the arrival of another Christmas, sit back and enjoy this book. We'll begin by traveling back in time to the origins of our Christmas traditions. Then we'll travel through modern-day Europe—from England to Norway, to France, Germany, and Austria, and then south to Italy, finishing in the Swiss Alps. Along the way we'll find Christmas customs that are both foreign and familiar, exploring new and different ways to celebrate the joy of the holidays.

THE ROOTS OF CHRISTMAS

MIDWINTER CELEBRATION: A PAGAN PARTY

FOR AS LONG as people have shivered in the winter, they have celebrated the beginning of its end. For the prehistoric people of Europe, midwinter was known as the Yuletide, meaning the "turning of the sun."

Imagine you're living in the cold of northern Europe before the birth of Christ. Your gods are the mysterious forces of nature—the sun, rain, and wind. In summer it's warm, plants grow, and food is plentiful. Then it gets cold and dark, and the earth becomes frozen and bleak.

The pre-Christian world was ruled by mysterious gods and the forces of nature.

Just when everything looks darkest—around December 21st, the winter solstice, the longest night of the year—what do you do? You throw a party! And, slowly but surely, the cycle turns. Your sun god, who'd been weak and sick, is now on the mend, spring is coming, and once again life is returning to your world.

For the prehistoric people of Europe, late December—though dreary and dark—was the perfect time to celebrate. Why? Because they had fresh meat and good grog to celebrate with: In December, villagers often slaughtered the cattle they couldn't afford to feed through the winter, so this was the only time of year when many of them had fresh meat. Also, wine and beer made earlier in the year had finally fermented and were ready to drink. Time to party!

CHRISTIANIZING THE WINTER FEST: FROM SUN WORSHIP TO SON WORSHIP

The pagan Romans conquered the pagan Celtic people around 50 B.C. The Romans called their solstice festival Saturnalia, and it was marked by feasting and good-natured goofiness. Then, as Christianity slowly spread through Rome—becoming the empire's chief religion by the fourth century A.D.—the midwinter celebration got a new twist.

In the first few centuries of Christianity, Easter was the primary holiday— Jesus' birthday wasn't even celebrated. (The Bible doesn't say exactly when Jesus was born, and what it does say—that "shepherds were herding their flocks"—suggests spring rather than winter.) But in the year 350, Pope Julius I decided to make the birth of Jesus a holiday, choosing December 25th.

Politically it was a clever choice, because the young religion (legal for less than a century) could then adopt and absorb the traditions of the immensely popular Saturnalia. The fun-loving spirit of the pagan festival dovetailed nicely with the joyous welcome given to the Christ child. By the mid-fifth century, the Feast of the Nativity, as Christmas was first called, was celebrated from Egypt to England.

CHRISTMAS: PARTY OR PRAY?

The "true" meaning of Christmas is tricky to determine. By the Middle Ages (A.D. 500–1500), Christianity had largely replaced pagan religions. But the

A pagan midwinter ritual is the centerpiece of this small-town Italian Christmas Eve celebration.

hedonistic partying of pre-Christian religions was inextricably woven into Christian celebrations. On Christmas, believers attended church, and then got wild and crazy.

Though church leaders would have preferred to celebrate with more reverence than revelry, pagan customs survived: People still sang in roving bands, shared bowls of wassail (spiced wine), performed farcical plays, and exchanged gifts at New Year. Most medieval lords provided a Christmas feast for their tenants and made the 12 days of Christmas a holiday from work, so for many people, Christmas was as much about feeding the body as feeding the soul. From these festive rituals, long celebrated around the winter Christian holy days, many sacred observances emerged that are still beloved by the faithful as integral parts of their Christmas celebrations.

In the later Middle Ages, as Europe's ethnic groups coalesced into nations, they took their Christmas customs in separate though often similar directions. In this book, as we travel through England, Norway, France, Germany, Austria, Italy, and the Swiss Alps, we'll survey the many traditional ways in which Europeans celebrate Christmas.

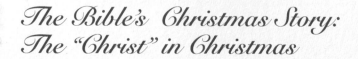

The Bible's Christmas Story: The "Christ" in Christmas

While each European culture gives Christmas its own special twist, they all follow the same story of how the son of God was born on Earth—as told in the Bible and illustrated over the centuries by great artists.

The Christmas story begins with the Annunciation: God sending an angel with a message for a young woman named Mary. And the angel said, "Fear not, for thou shalt bring forth a son, and you will name him Jesus. And he shall be called the Son of the Most High and his kingdom will have no end."

Detail from The Annunciation *(c. 1450–1453), Fra Filippo Lippi, courtesy of The National Gallery, London*

And it came to pass, that there went out a decree from Caesar Augustus, that all the world should be taxed. And Joseph, a carpenter from Nazareth, went with Mary, now expectant with child, to Bethlehem to be taxed.

Detail from Census at Bethlehem *(1566), Pieter Brueghel the Elder, courtesy of Musée des Beaux-Arts, Brussels*

And while they were there, she brought forth her firstborn son, wrapped him in swaddling clothes, and laid him in a manger, because there was no room in the inn.

Detail from The Nativity at Night *(late 15th century), Geertgen tot Sint Jans, courtesy of The National Gallery, London*

In that region there were shepherds keeping watch over their flocks by night. An angel of the Lord came to them, and said, "Fear not, for behold, I bring you tidings of great joy. For unto you is born on this day in the city of David a Savior, which is Christ the Lord."

Detail from The Adoration of the Shepherds *(1496), Luca Signorelli, courtesy of The National Gallery, London*

And suddenly a multitude of angels appeared, proclaiming: "Glory to God in the highest, and on Earth peace and goodwill to all people."

Detail from Mystic Nativity *(1500), Sandro Botticelli, courtesy of The National Gallery, London*

And the shepherds said, "Let us go to Bethlehem." There they found Mary, Joseph, and the babe lying in a manger.

Detail from The Adoration of the Shepherds *(1646), Rembrandt, courtesy of The National Gallery, London*

Now after Jesus was born, there also came Wise Men. And lo, the star, which they saw in the east, went before them, a beacon lighting the way to the Christ child.

Detail from The Adoration of the Kings *(1649), Carlo Dolci, courtesy of The National Gallery, London*

The Wise Men knelt down and worshipped the child, giving him gifts—gold, frankincense, and myrrh.

Detail from The Adoration of the Kings *(c. 1500), Vincenzo Foppa, courtesy of The National Gallery, London*

The long-awaited Messiah—meaning the "anointed one" in Hebrew—had arrived. The Greek word for anointed was *Xristos*, or Christ. The day people celebrated the Mass of the anointed king became Christ's Mass . . . Christmas.

Detail from The Adoration of the Kings *(1649), Carlo Dolci, courtesy of The National Gallery, London*

SO WHAT'S THE (REAL) STORY?

When it comes to the Christmas story, religious scholars—conservative, liberal, evangelical, feminist, and those in between—still discuss and dispute its most beloved elements. In fact, the part of Jesus' biography that church historians feel most uncertain about is the story of his birth. These aren't debates about the literal truth of the Gospels, since there's general consensus that the dramatic arc of Jesus' life story isn't based on physical evidence. Of the four Gospels, only the two written by Matthew and Luke contain accounts of that first Christmas, but these are contradictory. What scholars want to know is: What motivated Matthew and Luke to tell the story of the Nativity differently?

Detail from The Adoration of the Kings *(1649), Carlo Dolci, courtesy of The National Gallery, London*

For example, compare the different Annunciation scenes in these two Gospels. In Matthew's version, an angel reveals the news to Joseph, not Mary, that a special child will be born to his future wife, and does so through a dream: "Joseph, son of David, do not fear to take Mary your wife, for that which is conceived in her is of the Holy Spirit; and she will bear a son, and you shall call him Jesus, for he will save his people from their sins." Later, an angel appears again to Joseph in a dream (not to Mary), and tells him to flee with her and the baby to Egypt for safety.

In Luke's version (the more familiar one), the angel Gabriel appears directly to Mary and makes an elaborate and rather lengthy announcement: "Do not be afraid, Mary, for you have found favor with God. And behold, you will conceive in your womb and bear a son, and you shall call his name Jesus. He will be great, and will be called

Detail from The Annunciation *(late 15th century) Giannicola di Paolo, courtesy of The National Gallery, London*

the Son of the Most High; and the Lord God will give to him the throne of his father David, and he will reign over the house of Jacob forever; and of his kingdom there will be no end."

And Mary said to the angel, "How can this be, since I have no husband?"

And the angel said to her, "The Holy Spirit will come upon you, and the power of the Most High will overshadow you; therefore the child to be born will be called holy, the Son of God."

Both Matthew and Luke were scribes who must have passionately believed in the remarkable events they recorded. So why are the details of their stories different? Does this difference discredit the big story? Many historians point out that to really

Detail from The Annunciation *(late 15th century), Giannicola di Paolo, courtesy of The National Gallery, London*

Xmas is OK

While some believe that "Xmas" takes the "Christ" out of "Christmas," it's actually not the case at all. *X* was the ancient Greek abbreviation for the word "Christ." The word for "Christ" in Greek is *Xristos*. During the 16th century, Europeans began using *X*, the first initial of Christ's name, as shorthand for the word "Christ" in "Christmas." Although the early Christians understood this shorthand, later Christians mistook "Xmas" as a sign of disrespect.

understand written history, we have to examine the background of the authors, their motives, and the audience they were writing for. Perhaps Matthew and Luke were just taking different approaches to arrive at the same theological goal—to win converts to their fledgling Christian faith.

Matthew was raised as a Jew in a Jewish neighborhood at a time when Christianity was first spreading among the Jewish populace. He wrote his story down sometime after A.D. 60. The voice he uses is direct and plainspoken. Intended to strike a chord with a Jewish audience, his Gospel echoes stories from the Old Testament (and therefore also from the holy book of the Jews, the Torah), working in themes and symbols familiar to Jews.

The Joseph who has the prophetic dream in Matthew's Gospel would have made Jews recall another Joseph—the one from the Old Testament (with a Technicolor coat). That Joseph also had a dream from God that promised greatness, and the same instruction to move his family to Egypt for safety.

Luke, on the other hand, was a pagan convert writing for a Roman audience a decade or two after Matthew. His writing was flowery enough to flatter an emperor. At the time, there was a lot of sizzle in stories written about the pagan superheroes, leaders such as Alexander the Great and Emperor Augustus. In those epics, the hero is not heroic unless his birth is a miraculous one, hinting at the grandeur of his future accomplishments. Luke delivers a larger-than-life announcement in the flamboyant language reserved for the superheroes of the day. Using the literary conventions of their times, both Matthew and Luke effectively wrote reader-friendly accounts that were aimed at winning over two different audiences.

It's interesting stuff, but by putting Jesus' birth under the microscope of scholarly analysis we may be missing the point of the simple story. A young woman gives birth to a baby, the Son of God, in the humblest of settings. A beautiful star appears. Shepherds stand beside kings, and together they celebrate the birth of the child. It's a love story for the ages. And the heart of the matter—for Christians anyway—is that the old tale is so well-told and inscribed with meaning that the simple lessons it offers in grace, acceptance, and faith are more essential than the veracity of the details.

CHRISTMAS TRADITIONS

FROM PRE-CHRISTMAS TREE
TO O TANNENBAUM

THE CHRISTMAS TREE'S "roots" run deep into the origins of the midwinter celebration. When winter's gloom descended on ancient pre-Christians, they looked around and saw a few things that didn't die—evergreens. This seemed to promise that the warmth and fertility of summer would return. After they decorated their huts with holly, ivy, or laurel, they likely took a deep whiff . . . and dreamed of spring.

The mysterious Druids, the priests of the ancient Celts, adorned their temples with evergreens as a symbol of everlasting life. The Vikings of Scandinavia considered

Hanging ornaments from a tree is a tradition dating back centuries.

evergreens the favored plant of their sun god. In many regions, people believed that evergreens, especially mistletoe, which was considered a sacred plant, would keep away witches, ghosts, evil spirits, and illness.

The custom continued in Christian times, but it wasn't until about 500 years ago in Germany that the practice of decorating evergreen trees became a part of Christmas. These first trees were strewn with cookies, apples, nuts, and sugar sticks—which children eagerly raided. In the 1800s, when candles became affordable, the tree of lights arrived, and the tradition of the family gathering around the tree to exchange gifts was established.

Lutherans like to believe (wrongly, according to scholars) that Martin Luther, the 16th-century Protestant reformer, first added lighted candles to a tree. The story

Martin Luther didn't "invent" the lighted Christmas tree, but it first became popular in Germany in his day.

goes that when he was walking home one winter evening, composing a sermon, he was awed by the brilliance of stars twinkling amidst evergreens. To recapture the scene for his family, he erected a tree in the main room and wired its branches with lighted candles.

Christmas trees as we know them got a big boost in popularity in the mid-19th-century, after a London magazine showed Queen Victoria, Prince Albert, and their family gathered around a Christmas tree. Victoria was a favorite with her subjects, and what she did immediately became fashionable—not only in Britain, but in fashion-conscious East Coast American society as well. In the early 1900s, during the Art Nouveau age, trees began to be draped in tinsel and ornamented with lovingly painted glass bulbs. The Christmas tree had arrived.

Glittering glass ornaments attract shoppers in Germany's Christmas markets.

In Germany—the land of *O Tannenbaum*—Christmas trees became so popular that during World War I, thousands of them were actually mailed to soldiers on the Western Front. These tiny fake trees, made of feathers and paper, came in a kit, ready to be assembled right out of the postage box.

SANTA CLAUS: THE MANY FACES BEHIND THE BEARD

Our American Santa Claus—a plump, jolly old fellow dressed in red—is just one of many gift-giving characters who preside over the Christmas season. Depending on where you are in Europe, it's possible to bump into St. Nicholas, Father Christmas,

Whatever the name, a kindly man bringing gifts is a hit with kids.

Père Noël, Samichlaus, Sinterklaas, and others. All are brothers of sorts, tracing their lineage back either to an early Christian saint or a pagan deity. The origin of these multicultural gift-givers is a tangle of folklore, crossed with some early Christian public relations and a dash of modern commercial branding.

FATHER CHRISTMAS

Let's start with the branch of the family that hails from the frozen north. Long before the birth of Christ, there was Odin, father of the Viking gods. Like Santa, Odin was a stout old man dressed in furs with white hair and a long beard. During the winter solstice, Odin rode through the sky on his eight-legged magical horse, Sleipnir, and descended to earth. Disguised in a hooded cloak, he would eavesdrop on Vikings

In pagan times, the powerful gods came alive during the midwinter festival.

sitting around the campfire, trying to figure out who had been naughty and who had been nice. Occasionally, he would leave a gift of bread for a poor family.

Around the same time in the British Isles, chilly Celts were crowning a Frost King and appealing for leniency during the harsh midwinter months. In the Middle Ages, the legends of King Frost and Odin became associated with the Christian practice of helping the needy at Christmas. Parishes would hire actors in disguise to go undercover through the village, finding needy families, and reporting back to the village priest. In the 16th century, during the party-hearty reign of the Tudors, the character morphed into Captain Christmas, a sort of master of ceremonies presiding over the unruly fun at Christmastide. Banned by Puritan prudes in the 17th century, he re-emerged in the 18th century in plays put on by itinerant players as Father Christmas.

In the 19th-century Victorian era, Father Christmas was portrayed as a bearded pagan wearing robes and a crown of holly, ivy, or icicles, while hoisting a bowl of wassail. Gone were any saintly attributes, but he was a jolly enough fellow who made people happy during the dark days of winter—even if he drank a bit too much at the company Christmas party!

Toward the end of the 19th century, Father Christmas was reinvented as the bringer of gifts to children. This probably came about because of the Victorians' emerging interest in their children, coupled with influences from Europe and America, where St. Nicholas and Santa were popular.

Today, Father Christmas is a kind old gentleman who dresses, depending on his whim, in a long red robe trimmed with fur or a belted red jacket and cap (in which case he is easily confused with Santa, whose nocturnal habits he has also acquired).

ST. NICHOLAS

Meanwhile, another branch of the Santa Family tree was sprouting from an early Christian monk named St. Nicholas. It's believed that the historical Nicholas was born in the Eastern Roman Empire (now Turkey) sometime around A.D. 280. Some folklore experts have suggested his life story was probably recycled from tales of various pagan gods and then Christianized. Legends abound about St. Nicholas, who became the bishop of Myra (modern-day Damre, Turkey), and was much admired for his piety and kindness. He was rumored to have given away all of his inherited wealth to travel the countryside helping the poor and sick. He kept an especially watchful eye on orphans, occasionally giving them gifts; over the years, his reputation grew as a compassionate protector of children.

Samichlaus, a "descendant" of St. Nick, and his sidekick Schmutzli offer the carrot and the stick to keep kids in line.

According to one story, he prevented three poor sisters from being sold into prostitution by their destitute father. Nicholas provided them with a dowry, so they could be married. The legend grew that he gave the money anonymously by tossing bags of gold through a window, or perhaps down the chimney. The gold landed in the girls' stockings (some versions swap stockings for shoes) which had been left by the fire to dry.

By the Middle Ages, St. Nicholas was the most popular saint in Europe. On the eve of his Feast Day, December 6th (the anniversary of his death), a bearded, robed man appeared in every village, passing out gifts to children and the poor.

THE SANTA FAMILY

In many lands, there were now two Christmas figures—the Christian St. Nicholas (commemorated on December 5th and 6th) and the pagan party animal who became Father Christmas (December 24th, 25th, and beyond). Over the centuries, different cultures merged these two figures, some emphasizing one legend over the other, some celebrating on the 6th, some on the 25th, some both. Today, a European Christmas brings the whole extended Santa Family together.

In Switzerland, St. Nicholas became Samichlaus. With his henchman, Schmutzli, Samichlaus travels through alpine villages on a sure-footed donkey. In classic good cop/bad cop mode, Samichlaus brings the good kids delicious treats—tangerines, chocolates, gingerbread—while scary Schmutzli consults a big book of bad deeds and keeps a sack handy so he can take away the naughty children and eat them later (see photo at left).

In Finland, St. Nicholas acquired a few reindeer to help him in his travels (perhaps borrowed from the pagan god, Odin). In Norway, a cross between Father Christmas and a traditional Norwegian forest elf resulted in a pint-sized, long-bearded gift-giver known as the Julenisse.

France merged St. Nicholas with Father Christmas to get Père Noël. On December 25th, Père Noël travels in the company of Père Fouettard, a very bad butcher who once tried to pickle some children. Nicholas rescued them, and now Père Fouettard is doomed to follow around his better-behaved compatriot, helping deliver presents to French children.

The 16th-century German reformer, Martin Luther, wanted to shift the focus away from pagan revelry and legendary saints and back on the birthday boy, Jesus. So he attempted to swap (the Catholic) St. Nicholas for (the Protestant-friendly) Christkind, or Christ child, as the gift-giver. But German children had a tough time grasping that the baby Jesus actually brought presents, and over time, the Christ child morphed into an angel. In some legends, the Christkind became associated with a jolly old man named Kris Kringle. German immigrants exported this version to America, eventually fusing it with the gift-giving St. Nicholas to become the American Santa Claus. In Germany, the magic gift-giver—still called Christkind—became an angelic young girl who visits each Christmas with goodies.

The Christkind eventually caught on, but many parents today ignore Luther's wishes anyway, so plenty of German kids get the best of both worlds—gifts from St. Nicholas on December 6th and from the Christkind on the 25th. St. Nick fills shoes that kids have left out with chocolates, oranges, and nuts. His grumpy sidekick, Knecht Ruprecht, leaves bundles of twigs for children listed in his black book.

In the Netherlands, St. Nicholas became the main man, known as Sinterklaas. He arrives dressed like a bishop, in a red robe, mitered hat, and shepherd's staff, carrying a large book with the names of the good and bad kids. On December 5th, he travels the countryside with his sidekick, a dark-skinned mischief-maker named Zwarte Piet

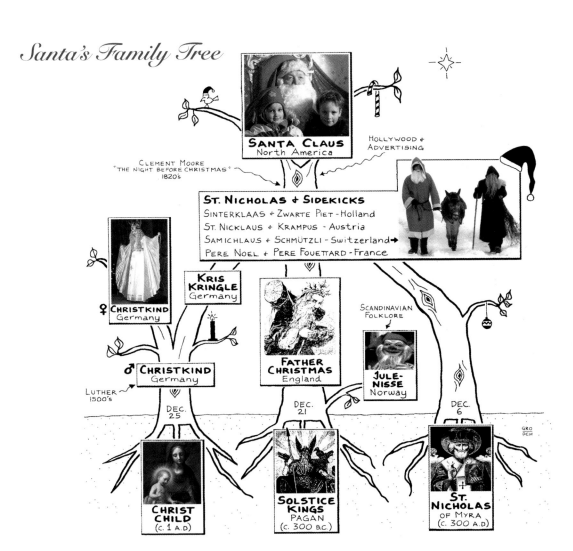

Santa's Family Tree

SANTA CLAUS
North America

HOLLYWOOD &
ADVERTISING

CLEMENT MOORE
"THE NIGHT BEFORE CHRISTMAS"
1820's

ST. NICHOLAS & SIDEKICKS
SINTERKLAAS & ZWARTE PIET - Holland
ST. NICKLAUS & KRAMPUS - Austria
SAMICHLAUS & SCHMÜTZLI - Switzerland →
PERE NOEL & PERE FOUETTARD - France

♀ **CHRISTKIND**
Germany

KRIS KRINGLE
Germany

♂ **CHRISTKIND**
Germany

LUTHER
1500's

FATHER CHRISTMAS
England

SCANDINAVIAN
FOLKLORE

JULE-NISSE
Norway

DEC.
25

DEC.
21

DEC.
6

GRO
DCH

CHRIST CHILD
(C. 1 A.D)

SOLSTICE KINGS
PAGAN
(C. 300 B.C.)

ST. NICHOLAS
OF MYRA
(C. 300 A.D)

(Black Peter), who hefts a burlap sack of candy and gifts. During the night, Zwarte Piet climbs down chimneys to leave presents in good kids' shoes. Today, many Dutch also celebrate Christmas on the 25th.

AMERICA'S SANTA CLAUS

Early American settlers had strong ties with the Christmas traditions of England. In the 17th century, Dutch immigrants brought the story of St. Nicholas to America. Americans loved the custom, but had trouble pronouncing the name. "Sinterklaas" became "Santa Claus," and the name stuck. Our modern Santa Claus is an amalgam of European traditions, combining the kindly, gift-giving St. Nicholas and the mischievous, fun-loving Father Christmas.

In 1822, Clement Clark Moore, a professor of classics at the General Theological Seminary in New York City, wrote a poem for his six children on Christmas Eve, which he called *A Visit From Saint Nicholas* (later known as *The Night Before Christmas*). Whether by design or intention, or perhaps because he was writing for the delight of his own children, Moore transformed the patron saint of children into a fairy-tale figure that kids could finally love.

A Visit from Saint Nicholas

BY CLEMENT CLARKE MOORE

'Twas the night before Christmas, when all through the house
Not a creature was stirring, not even a mouse;
The stockings were hung by the chimney with care,
In hopes that St. Nicholas soon would be there;
The children were nestled all snug in their beds,
While visions of sugar-plums danced in their heads;
And mamma in her 'kerchief, and I in my cap,
Had just settled our brains for a long winter's nap,
When out on the lawn there arose such a clatter,
I sprang from the bed to see what was the matter.
Away to the window I flew like a flash,
Tore open the shutters and threw up the sash.
The moon on the breast of the new-fallen snow
Gave the luster of mid-day to objects below,
When, what to my wondering eyes should appear,
But a miniature sleigh, and eight tiny reindeer,
With a little old driver, so lively and quick,
I knew in a moment it must be St. Nick.

More rapid than eagles his coursers they came,
And he whistled, and shouted, and called them by name;
"Now, Dasher! now, Dancer! now, Prancer and Vixen!
On, Comet! on, Cupid! on, Donder and Blitzen!
To the top of the porch! to the top of the wall!
Now dash away! dash away! dash away all!"
As dry leaves that before the wild hurricane fly,
When they meet with an obstacle, mount to the sky;
So up to the house-top the coursers they flew,
With the sleigh full of toys, and St. Nicholas too.
And then, in a twinkling, I heard on the roof
The prancing and pawing of each little hoof.
As I drew in my head, and was turning around,
Down the chimney St. Nicholas came with a bound.
He was dressed all in fur, from his head to his foot,
And his clothes were all tarnished with ashes and soot;
A bundle of toys he had flung on his back,
And he looked like a peddler just opening his pack.
His eyes—how they twinkled! his dimples how merry!
His cheeks were like roses, his nose like a cherry!
His droll little mouth was drawn up like a bow
And the beard of his chin was as white as the snow;

The stump of a pipe he held tight in his teeth,
And the smoke it encircled his head like a wreath;
He had a broad face and a little round belly,
That shook when he laughed, like a bowlful of jelly.
He was chubby and plump, a right jolly old elf,
And I laughed when I saw him, in spite of myself;
A wink of his eye and a twist of his head,
Soon gave me to know I had nothing to dread;
He spoke not a word, but went straight to his work,
And filled all the stockings; then turned with a jerk,
And laying his finger aside of his nose,
And giving a nod, up the chimney he rose;
He sprang to his sleigh, to his team gave a whistle,
And away they all flew like the down of a thistle,
But I heard him exclaim, ere he drove out of sight,
"Happy Christmas to all, and to all a good night."

Today's image of the American Santa Claus—the jolly fellow with the apple cheeks and twinkling eyes—came by way of a German immigrant who published his illustrations in *Harper's Weekly* in the late 1800s. This magnanimous Santa Claus was a boon to shopkeepers during a period of unprecedented growth in retailing— department stores, chain stores, and new-fangled billboards. They joyfully exploited the commercial potential of an entire season dedicated to gift giving, brought to you by Santa. In the 1930s, the Coca Cola Company, in need of a sales boost, borrowed Santa's image and branded their product with the merry ol' gent . . . thus completing his epic journey from saint to salesman.

Today, in many parts of Europe, there's a movement to preserve the tradition of St. Nicholas, who's at risk of being crowded out by the American Santa. Some villages are even creating Santa-free zones. They see Santa as a super-size symbol of consumption. St. Nicholas, they argue, embodies the real Christmas spirit, a monk whose example taught that giving doesn't make us poorer—it makes us richer.

The Christmas countdown begins with Advent.

CHRISTMAS:
NOT A DAY BUT A SEASON

In the seven European countries we'll visit on our journey, Christmas is more than just December 25th—it's a season that lasts for more than a month. This isn't so people have more time to shop, but to fit in all of the holy days and festivals.

First comes Advent, the time to anticipate the "arrival" (advent) of the baby Jesus. Advent begins four Sundays before Christmas Eve. (In Europe, this is truly the start of Christmas, since advertisers are reluctant to commercialize the season any earlier.) Next up is the Feast of St. Nicholas, celebrated mostly in Catholic countries with lots of gift giving on the eve or day of December 6th. In some countries, St. Nicholas'

Santa Lucia Day, December 13, is just one of many holidays in a month of merrymaking.

Feast is even bigger than Christmas Day. December 13th brings Santa Lucia Day, a highlight in Scandinavia, when young girls decked out in candles lead processions promising the return of the light.

For many Europeans, Christmas Eve is the main event, celebrated with Midnight Mass and a grand meal. Others concentrate on the family time and gift giving of Christmas Day. But for those who really get into the holiday spirit, December 25th is just the start. The Twelve Days of Christmas—featuring more parties, gift giving, and the ringing in of the New Year—stretch from December 25th until January 5th. This period is followed by Epiphany, the day the Three Kings delivered their gifts. The Christmas season finally goes into hibernation after this . . . at least until next year.

Whew! That's a lot of celebrating, so we'd better get started. And what better place to begin making merry than in merry olde England? Cheers!

ENGLAND

Happy Christmas!

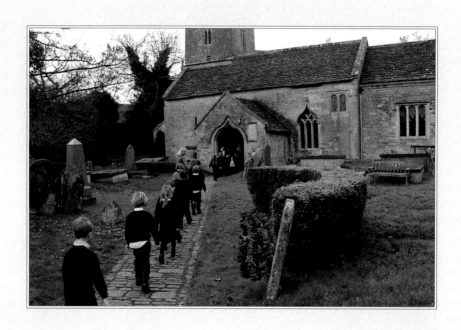

Some say that ever 'gainst that season comes
Wherein our Savior's birth is celebrated,
The bird of dawning singeth all night long:
And then, they say, no spirit dare stir abroad,
The nights are wholesome, then no planets strike,
No fairy takes nor witch hath power to charm,
So hallow'd and so gracious is the time.

—WILLIAM SHAKESPEARE,
Hamlet, Act 1, Scene 1

AN ELIZABETHAN CHRISTMAS

MANY OF OUR CLASSIC Christmas traditions—holly, mistletoe, caroling, and the Christmas feast—have been celebrated in England for centuries.

In England, the Christmas season, or Christmastide, lasts from December 24th to January 6th, Epiphany. During the time of Queen Elizabeth I (1533–1603), Christmastide was celebrated with an extravagant hospitality that extended to the whole household—whether manor, village, or court. The wealthy loaded their tables with all the meats and mince pies they could afford and invited everyone to the party—from aristocratic families and courtiers to the lowliest workers.

Christmastide began by crowning a master of ceremonies for the Twelve Days of Christmas—the Lord of Misrule, often a student or beggar. The Lord then chose his

Court of Misrule, usually eager partiers, to help him manage his unruly business—feasting, games, and dancing. During these topsy-turvy times, the poor descended on the rich, demanding their best food and drink. If owners failed to comply, they were terrorized with mischief. Christmas became the time of year when the upper classes could repay their (real or imagined) debt to society by entertaining less fortunate citizens.

The festival raged into the New Year. Despite some religious holy days, the celebration was quite secular, featuring masked balls, plays, dancing, eating and drinking, gift-giving, gambling, lots of cards, and general carnival-like craziness. It culminated with the biggest bash on January 5th, the Twelfth Night.

As in Elizabethan times, Christmas today can be a bit raucous and unruly.

CHRISTMAS CAROLING

The joy of Christmas poured out in song. The caroling season traditionally stretched from St. Thomas' Day (December 21st) to Christmas morning. In medieval times, carols were not just songs but also folk dances, performed by wandering musicians accompanied by singers. Considered a pagan holdover, carol singers were banned from church, so instead they'd go door to door visiting the homes of the big shots, performing in hopes of getting a coin, meal, drink, or Christmas treat.

The spirit of an English Christmas abides in song, and even today, towns everywhere are alive with music. From street-corner buskers to sublime choral groups, the English sing their hearts out at Christmas.

Fun and Games

Elizabethans loved to play games, especially at Christmas. Here are a few of their favorites:

Snapdragon:
Players take turns picking raisins out of a dish of flaming brandy and popping them into their mouth. Ouch! Players bet on each other's chances of success.

King of the Bean:
On Twelfth Day a bean is baked into a cake. Pieces of cake are distributed among the children and servants. The lucky one who finds the bean is pronounced King of the Bean, and reigns supreme for the rest of the day and night. Sometimes a pea is used as well, and whoever finds it becomes the Queen of the Pea.

Fortune-Telling:
On Christmas Eve young girls try to divine which one of them will get married first.

The Twelve Days of Christmas:
It's thought that the Christmas carol starring "a partridge in a pear tree" originated with a memory game played on Twelfth Night. Each player sang a verse in turn, adding a new gift while trying to remember all the earlier ones as they sang their way through the list.

FEASTING

In about 1570 a proper English Christmas feast was described in this way:

Good husband and housewife, now chiefly be glad,
Things handsome to have, as they ought to be had.
They both do provide, against Christmas do come,
To welcome their neighbors, good cheer to have some.

Good bread and good drink, a good fire in the hall,
Brawn, pudding, and souse, and good mustard withal.
Beef, mutton, and pork, and good pies of the best,
Pig, veal, goose, and capon, and turkey well drest,
Cheese, apples, and nuts, and good carols to hear,
As then in the country is counted good cheer.

What cost to good husband, is any of this?
Good household provision only it is:
Of other the like, I do leave out a many,
That costeth the husband never a penny.
—THOMAS TUSSER

The high point of Christmastide was the feasting, which in part served as a reminder that the ever-present threat of hunger had been triumphantly overcome. One notable Christmas celebration was rumored to have featured a giant 165-pound pie that was nine feet in diameter. Its ingredients included two bushels of flour, 20 pounds of butter, four geese, two rabbits, four wild ducks, two woodcocks, six snipes, four partridges, two curlews, six pigeons, and seven blackbirds.

With as many as 24 courses, guests could count on traditional goodies such as mince pies, frumenty (sweet, spiced mush), plum pudding, and humble pie. Humble (or 'umble) pie was made from the "humbles," or innards, of a deer. While the lords and ladies ate the finer cuts, servants baked the humbles into a pie for themselves. And plum pudding had nothing to do with plums. It was a mixture of suet, flour, sugar, raisins, nuts, and spices tied loosely in cloth and boiled until the ingredients were "plum," or swollen enough to fill the cloth. During the Puritan reign, plum pudding was deemed "sinfully rich" and outlawed.

The sweetmeat or dessert course allowed a host to show off his wealth and status— classic conspicuous consumption. Sweetmeats decorated with crystallized fruits and gold leaf made a splendid presentation. Sugar, which was expensive, was a featured ingredient. The mistress of the house tried to dazzle the guests with her culinary wit and artistry. Creative cooks were especially fond of a concoction of egg, sugar, and gelatin, which they could mold into almost any form imaginable.

MINCE PIE

In Britain, eating mince pie at Christmas dates back to the 16th century, or earlier. Some believe that the idea originated with the gifts that were brought to baby Jesus. It's not too hard to imagine dried fruits, nuts, and spices being presented to the child, alongside gold, frankincense, and myrrh.

In the Middle Ages, a mince pie was made in a big dish and called a "Christmas pye." A standard pye recipe called for "a most learned mixture of Neats-tongue (ox tongue), chicken, eggs, sugar, raisins, lemon, and orange peel, various kinds of spicery . . ."

Eventually, little tarts in the shape of a cradle took the place of the great big pie.

Sometimes a small figure was tucked underneath the crust to represent the baby Jesus. By the 16th century, mince or shred pies (a reference to the shredded meat that was mixed with chopped egg and ginger) had become a Christmas specialty. Over time the recipe was fancied up with dried fruit and other sweets, and by the 17th century, the filling closely resembled today's mix of suet, spices, and dried fruit steeped in brandy.

While Americans bake their mince pies bigger, the traditional English pie is a cute little one-serving goodie. It's customary to have a mince pie or two in the pantry to offer to an unexpected guest. And if offered a pie, it's considered rude not to accept.

When making a mince pie, superstition dictates that everyone must take a turn stirring the filling and making a wish. Always stir in a clockwise direction, the direction

The traditional mince pie is a one-serving goodie filled with shredded, sugared nostalgia.

Maddy's Marvelous Mince Pies

(Makes 12 individual pies)

For the orange pastry:

2 sticks (8 ounces) chilled, unsalted butter
½ cup vegetable shortening
4 cups self-rising flour (or 4 cups all-purpose flour
    mixed with 1 T. baking powder and ½ t. salt)
2 ½ T. caster sugar (finely ground) or granulated sugar
Grated zest and juice of one large orange

For the filling:

1 8-ounce package of cream cheese, softened
⅓ cup caster sugar or granulated sugar
2 cups prepared mincemeat (look for it at the grocery,
    British import stores, or online)
1 large egg, beaten, or 3 T. milk

To make the orange pastry: Using a pastry cutter or two knives, cut the butter and shortening into the flour in a large bowl until the mixture resembles coarse breadcrumbs. Stir in the sugar and orange zest and add the juice by tablespoons until the mixture comes together. Gather into a ball, wrap in plastic wrap and refrigerate for at least 30 minutes.

To make the filling: Using an electric mixer on medium speed, beat the cream cheese and sugar together until light, about three to four minutes. Set aside.

Preheat the oven to 400°F. Lightly grease a standard 12-compartment muffin pan.

Divide the pastry dough in half. Take one half and roll it out on a lightly-floured board until about ¼-inch in thickness. Cut twelve 6-inch rounds and fit them into the bottoms and up the sides of the muffin compartments.

Dollop the mincemeat into the pastry, dividing equally. Top with the cream cheese mixture. Roll out the remaining pastry and cut out twelve 3 ½-inch rounds. Brush the edges of the pastry in the muffin tins with the beaten egg or milk, then place the 3 ½-inch rounds on top. Pinch the rounds together to seal them securely.

Bake 20 minutes or until pastry is lightly browned on top. Let cool in the pan and then turn out.

in which the sun would have circled an earth once thought to be at the center of the universe. To stir the other way could spell big trouble in the coming year. Once it's baked, make a wish on the first pie of the season, and then eat a pie for each of the Twelve Days of Christmas. This will bring 12 happy months in the year to follow.

WASSAIL & WASSAILING

Wassail was a type of spiced wine or ale drunk at Christmas. If you were an olde Englishman drinking wassail, you would say to your companions, "Waes hail!" meaning, "May you be healthy!" The proper response? "Drink hail!" or "Drink good health!"

Whether served in a Viking drinking horn or a paper cup, hot spiced drinks warm the soul.

Eat, Drink, and be Merry

You're celebrating Christmas in 1625. Pour yourself a mug of spiced ale, dig into a piece of mince pie, and sing this rhyme:

> *So now is come our joyful'st feast,*
> *Let every man be jolly.*
> *Each room with ivy leaves is drest,*
> *And every post with holly.*
> *Though some churls at our mirth repine,*
> *'Round your foreheads garlands twine,*
> *Drown sorrow in a cup of wine,*
> *And let us all be merry.*
> —George Wither (1588–1667)

The process of mulling or simmering wine with spices can be traced back to Roman times, when winemaking included the addition of salt, myrtle, juniper, honey, rose petals, and citrus rinds. It's thought that honey and spices were added to a simmering pot of wine in the Middle Ages to mask its bitter tannins. In merry—but chilly—olde England, they heated it up and served it during Christmastide. The English have been drinking it during the winter holidays ever since.

Wassailing was more than just drinking. In town, groups of maidens went door to door with an empty cup or wassail bowl asking the master of a house to fill it with spiced ale (or cake, cheese, or a silver penny). The wassailing wenches, who sang a little ditty, were always welcomed into the house, where they'd drink to the host's health. To refuse them was to refuse the good fortune they brought. The tendency to confuse wassailing with caroling (as in "Here we come a-wassailing . . .") comes from this custom of singing songs and drinking from the wassail bowl.

WASSAILING RHYMES & CHANTS

Wassaile the trees, that they might beare
Many a plum and many a peare:
For more or lesse fruits they will bring,
As you do give them wassailing.

Huzza, Huzza, in our good town
The bread shall be white, and the liquor be brown
So here my old fellow I drink to thee
And the very health of each other tree.
Well may ye blow, well may ye bear
Blossom and fruit both apple and pear.
So that every bough and every twig
May bend with a burden both fair and big
May ye bear us and yield us fruit such a store
That the bags and chambers and house run o'er.

In the countryside, wassailing was a ceremony which involved blessing the land and drinking to the health of crops and animals, especially apple trees. Groups of young men went between orchards performing a rite known as "howling an orchard" for a reward. It's likely the custom descended directly from pagan practices.

For an authentic cup of wassail, here's a 17th-century recipe that comes from a poem about Twelfth Night festivities. (Note: "Lamb's wooll" refers to the soft, fluffy white pulp spooned from a roasted crab apple.)

Next crowne the bowle full
With gentle lamb's wooll;
Adde sugar, nutmeg and ginger,
With store of ale too;
And thus ye must doe
To make a Wassaile a swinger.
—ROBERT HERRICK

On Elizabethan farms, "wassailing" meant roaming the fields from farm to farm, drinking to the health of the crops.

MISTLETOE AND CHRISTMAS GREENS: OF CELTS AND KISSING

During the Christmastide festivities, houses were decorated with anything that was still green in December—holly, ivy, yew, bay, laurel, and mistletoe. Since pagan times, evergreens were valued for their ability to remain green in the winter, and in some species, to produce berries or flowers. The mysterious Druids, the priestly class of the Celtic peoples living in England (c. 500 B.C.), were devout nature worshippers. During the winter solstice, the Druids decorated their temples with winter-bearing holly and mistletoe, which were considered sacred. The Celtic name for mistletoe means "all healer," and it was thought to be a remedy against poison and

Holly, one of the few plants bearing fruit in winter, holds the promise of new life.

to make barren animals fertile. For pagans, bringing greens inside ensured fertility and warded off evil spirits. For Christians, who adopted the practice, living greens symbolized the everlasting life guaranteed through Christ and reminded them that even in the hardest, darkest times, faith does not die.

It's hard to know how the (mostly English) custom of kissing under the mistletoe came about, but we do know the Druids believed that the spirit of fertility stirred in the sacred bough. The tradition is likely a vestige of those wild days—and nights—of the winter solstice celebrations. By the 19th-century Victorian era, proper young men plucked a berry from the bough each time they kissed a girl. When the berries were all picked, the privilege ceased. Wherever it came from, it's still a handy excuse to steal a little Christmas kiss. And these days, there's no berry-related limit.

Today, mistletoe offers an excuse to share a smooch.

Mistletoe

Sitting under the mistletoe
(Pale-green, fairy mistletoe),
One last candle burning low,
All the sleepy dancers gone,
Just one candle burning on,
Shadows lurking everywhere:
Some one came, and kissed me there.

Tired I was; my head would go
Nodding under the mistletoe
(Pale-green, fairy mistletoe),
No footsteps came, no voice, but only,
Just as I sat there, sleepy, lonely,
Stooped in the still and shadowy air
Lips unseen—and kissed me there.

—WALTER DE LA MARE (1873–1956)

The YULE LOG

On Christmas Eve, young men would ceremoniously carry a massive log from the forest to the hearth, to burn through the Christmas season. This Yule log had its origins with pre-Christian Northerners, both the Druids and Norsemen of Scandinavia. In the darkest days of the year, during winter solstice festivities, they set the great log on fire. It burned day and night, protecting them from winter's cold-hearted demons and calling back the light and warmth of the sun. In medieval times, the log burned continuously for the 12 nights of revelry during Christmastide. Once the fire died, a bit of the charred wood was saved to light the next winter's log, symbolizing the continuity of life.

In one of those "if you can't beat 'em, join 'em" moves, the Christian church co-opted this pagan tradition to honor Jesus, known as the light of the world. Today, Christians continue to celebrate the triumph over darkness with candlelight services.

The ORIGINAL GRINCH

More mischief in that time committed than in all the year besides . . .
What dicing and carding, what eating and drinking, what banqueting and feasting
is then used . . . to the great dishonour of God and the impoverishing of the realm.

Such were the pray-don't-party sentiments of one Philip Stubbes in the late 16th century. Stubbes spoke for the powerful few who ruled England in the Puritan (strict Protestant) heyday. For some time, the rowdy approach to Christmas had troubled the church. They felt the holiday had become dangerous—an excuse for all sorts of bad behavior. Something, they surmised, must be done.

Which is why Oliver Cromwell (1599–1658)—a commoner who beheaded the king and briefly ruled England—gets my vote for the original Grinch. In the 17th century, Cromwell and his Puritan forces—vowing to rid England of decadence—canceled Christmas. Cromwell preached against "the heathen traditions" of Christmas carols, decorated trees, and any joyful expression that desecrated "that sacred event." In 1644 an Act of Parliament banned all celebrations of the holiday, including attending church.

Christmas effectively went underground for the next 16 years. When the English deposed Cromwell in 1660 and put a king back on the throne, they promptly restored the holiday. Thereafter the observance of Christmas in England stumbled along, until the Victorians arrived on the scene and put the joy back into the season.

Under the Puritan Oliver Cromwell, Christmas cheer was silenced.

A VICTORIAN CHRISTMAS

... the only time I know of in the long calendar of the year, when men and women seem by one consent to open their shut-up hearts freely, and to think of other people below them as if they really were fellow-passengers to the grave, and not another race of creatures bound on other journeys. —CHARLES DICKENS

There's an impression that Christmas was "invented" during the reign of Queen Victoria (1839–1901). What the Victorians really did was to revive and reinvent the holiday. They took all that was best from Christmas past and adapted it to a fast-changing world. The Industrial Revolution was in full swing, bringing smoke-belching factories, overcrowded cities, stressed-out workers, and extreme poverty in the lower classes. Newly urbanized Victorians had a bad case of big-city blues.

"Hear ye, hear ye, let the festivities begin!"

Boxing Day

The day after Christmas is known in England and Canada as Boxing Day or St. Stephen's Day. On Boxing Day in Victorian England, affluent and middle-class families gave their servants Christmas boxes filled with tips and gifts—along with the day off (the only one of the year), so they could visit their families. Charitable Victorians would also distribute boxes filled with food and money to the poor of their parishes. Some received money in little pots with a slit in the top, which had to be smashed to get the money out. These small pots, nicknamed "piggies," became the original piggy banks.

Even Christmas—the year's only legal holiday—was in danger of being turned into another workday, under pressure from factory owners. ("You'll want all day tomorrow, I suppose?" says miserly Scrooge to poor, tired Bob Cratchit on Christmas Eve.) It seemed that capitalism might finally accomplish what the Puritans had not.

The Victorians yearned for something more meaningful. Looking back, they found much to admire in the way the Elizabethans had celebrated Christmas. They revived many of the "olde" traditions: burning the Yule log, decorating with fragrant winter greens, feasting, caroling, and general merrymaking.

Many in the middle class, having risen from poor circumstances, were anxious to maintain their social status, but were feeling guilty about having achieved it. Perhaps to assuage their guilt, they tried to fashion a Christmas that was morally and socially better than the Scrooge-like world that oppressed the poor around them. They decided that the true spirit of Christmas—and of Christianity—was about taking responsibility for those less fortunate. And so, charity and goodwill toward all became essential parts of Christmas.

The VICTORIAN TREE

The custom of decorating a fir tree at Christmas came to England by way of Germany. Queen Victoria and her German husband, Albert, were popular royals and trendsetters. In 1848, when the queen and her family were depicted in the *Illustrated London News* standing around a stylish Christmas tree, everyone wanted one.

Stalking, catching, and bringing home the perfect tree.

Christmas Cards

Sir Henry Cole was stressed out. It was Christmas of 1843, and he was a busy man, falling behind on his correspondence. It was common in 19th-century England to write seasonal messages to one's personal and business acquaintances on calling cards. Cole had an idea. He hired London artist John Calcott Horsley to design a Christmas card with a pre-written message, and mass-produced it on a printing press, creating the world's first commercial card.

That first Christmas card said, "Merry Christmas and a happy New Year to you" beneath a drawing of a family toasting an absent friend with glasses of wine. Along the sides were depicted charitable acts of clothing the naked and feeding the hungry. Family, good works, good eating and drinking—all the elements of a classic Victorian Christmas—were there on the card, along with a tiny blank space for Cole to sign his name. Newly efficient post offices in England and the United States made the cards nearly overnight sensations. Of the original one thousand cards printed for Henry Cole, only 12 exist today.

For more than a century, Christmas cards have helped loved ones keep in touch.

Victorians decorated their trees with homemade ornaments. Young ladies quilted snowflakes and stars and sewed small pouches for secret hanging gifts. Lighted candles, candies, and cakes were hung with ribbons and paper chains. Angel tree-toppers and fine silver tinsel imported from Germany provided the finishing touches.

DICKENS' A CHRISTMAS CAROL

Charles Dickens (1812–1870), author of the still much-loved *A Christmas Carol*, first published in 1843, captured the hearts and minds of Victorian England. Dickens' most enduring gift is a vivid expression of the social concerns of his time, and the book's message—the importance of charity and goodwill to all humankind—strikes a powerful chord.

Today's Tiny Tims celebrate the best Christmas ever.

Dickens, having been forced into the workforce as a child, was an especially compassionate observer of the plight of the children of London's poor. It's estimated that, in 1839, nearly half of all funerals in London were for children under the age of 10. Many who survived grew up without education, pressed into factory work with little chance of escaping the cycle of poverty. Dickens felt that the way to break the cycle was through education, which he championed in his writing.

Despite the availability of Ragged Schools—free schools run through charity—most poor children remained uneducated due to the demand for child labor. Compulsory education for all finally came in 1870, the year of Dickens' death.

CHILDREN: INVENTED BY VICTORIANS?

The idea of childhood as we know it really originated in the mid-1800s. Victorians, though strict, were far more sensitive to the emotional needs of children than their predecessors. Christmas, in particular, provided families with a day when they could lavish attention—and gifts—on their children without appearing to spoil them.

Victorians began to center Christmas on the family. Their role model was Queen Victoria and her husband, Prince Albert, who took great delight in ordinary domestic life and in raising their nine children. Where earlier, children were supposed to be seen but not heard, now they became part of the festivities, and people gathered together with all of their relatives. The Christmas crèche—showing Mary, Joseph, and baby Jesus together as the Holy Family—became a focal point of worship.

From Dickens' A Christmas Carol

It is good to be children sometimes,
and never better than at Christmas,
when its mighty Founder
was a child himself.

Puny Pete? Charles Dickens knew he'd need a cute little waif for his
story, but couldn't decide between Little Larry, Puny Pete, and
Small Sam. Then it came to him . . . Tiny Tim!

CHRISTMAS CRACKERS!

If there is one thing inseparable from Christmas in general and the little ones'
seasonable gathering in particular, it is—a cracker. With what a delightful look
of expectation they have waited for it to go "bang," and how they have screamed as
they scrambled after the surprise which came in response to the explosion...

This was how one Victorian writer described the tradition, beloved by children, of
pulling crackers. The Christmas cracker was invented by Tom Smith, an enterprising
London confectioner, in 1846. On a quick trip to the Continent, Tom discovered
pretty bonbons wrapped in tissue paper. Back in London, he decided his sweets
could use a twist of fancy tissue, too. These were popular, but Tom wasn't satisfied.

A traditional cracker puts the pop into Christmas.

A Sad Christmas March

In Victorian England, turkeys and geese were popular for Christmas dinners. Some of the birds were raised in Norfolk, and actually marched to market in London. To protect their feet from the frozen mud of the road, the turkeys were equipped with little leather boots. The geese, apparently lower on the pecking order, got only a coat of tar to protect their feet.

For seven years, he worked to develop something more spectacular. It came to him one night as he sat watching a crackling fire. What if he could make a bonbon that exploded with a pop? Eureka! Clever Tom took a strip of paper impregnated with chemicals which, when rubbed, created enough friction to produce a pop. He tucked it inside a colored paper wrapper and stuffed the wrapper with sweets, tiny toys, and love notes. The English have been popping Christmas crackers ever since.

VICTORIAN EDIBLES: The CHRISTMAS FEAST

After attending church, the highlight of Christmas Day in Victorian England was dinner and the festivities that followed—fireworks, songs, and games. Dinner was a sumptuous affair. There was fowl of some kind—a plump goose or turkey. Standing rib roast, a boar's head, a pork leg, oysters, mince pie, and plum pudding were big favorites, too.

PLUM PUDDING

The presentation of the plum pudding was a Christmas ritual. On "Stir-up Sunday," at the beginning of Advent, each member of the family took a turn at mixing the pudding and making a wish. Then a few tiny trinkets or silver coins were tossed in the batter. (These days, most people just pop a sixpence in their "puds," but miniature, traditional charms can still be purchased: a silver coin promises wealth in the coming year, a thimble ensures thrift, an anchor assures safety, and a tiny wishbone brings good luck.)

For the next few weeks, the pudding hung from a sack. On Christmas Day it was boiled in broth for eight hours, until it was fully "plum" (swollen). Just before

More than just a delicious dessert, the plum pudding is an annual ritual.

serving, it was doused with brandy, topped with a sprig of mistletoe, lit on fire, and carried to the table with great fanfare.

CHRISTMAS IN BRITAIN TODAY

Despite the onslaught of American-style commercialism, people in Britain today celebrate Christmas with many of the same traditions that were popular with their Elizabethan and Victorian forebears. Children remain the focal point of Christmas. They help choose and decorate the tree—often with ornaments they've made themselves—sing heartily at church concerts, act like perfect angels in school Nativity plays, or shout with glee at traditional holiday "panto" shows that feature popular fairy tales.

English children carefully decorate "biscuits" to hang on the tree.

Catherine's Christmas Pudding

(Makes 2 puddings, 1 pound each)

2 cups raisins

2 cups golden raisins

2 cups currants

1 ½ cups candied peel

3 cups beef suet, finely chopped

3 large eggs

3 cups fresh breadcrumbs

1 ½ cups lightly-packed brown sugar

2 cups self-rising flour

½ t. cinnamon

¼ t. salt

¼ t. nutmeg

⅛ t. ground cloves

⅛ t. allspice

½ cup finely ground almonds

10 oz. strong ale
  (Guinness works great!)

4 ½ t. double brandy

In a large bowl, mix the fruit, candied peel, suet, eggs, breadcrumbs, and sugar. In a separate bowl, blend together the flour, cinnamon, salt, nutmeg, cloves, allspice, and almonds. In a small bowl, stir together the ale and brandy. Add the flour mixture and ale mixture to the fruit. Mix well to achieve a cake-like consistency. Add more beer if too dry.

Grease two pudding pans (2-lb capacity apiece). Fill the pans, leaving a 1-inch space at the top. Cover with parchment or wax paper and tie it around the tops with cotton string.

Place in a steamer and steam for eight hours, refilling with more water as needed. Let cool completely. Replace the paper on top when cooled.

When cooked, the pudding should be a dark brown color and have a dense, spongy appearance. It's best to let it rest, then reheat it before serving on Christmas Day. To reheat, steam for 30 minutes to heat through.

This pudding will keep for about a year or so. From time to time, uncover, poke a skewer into the pudding in several places, and moisten generously with brandy.

Some children send letters to Father Christmas (or Santa), telling him what they want for Christmas. Some letters go by post or e-mail, but the more traditional way is to throw them into the back of the fireplace. The draft carries the letters up the chimney to Father Christmas. With naughty/nice list in hand, Father Christmas reads the letters and determines what each child will receive.

Late in the afternoon on Christmas Eve, many English families gather around the radio to listen to a carol service broadcast live from the Chapel of King's College in Cambridge. The service, first broadcast in 1928, has been heard on the radio in Britain every year since, including during World War II, when the ancient glass had to be removed from the Chapel and the College could not be identified for security reasons.

Shoppers at Christmasy Covent Garden will find classic toys for tots at Benjamin Pollock's famous toy shop, in business since the 1880s.

Just before bed, children set out a snack for Father Christmas—a sip of sherry, a mince pie, and carrots for the reindeer—and hang their stockings by the fireplace or at the foot of the bed. While they sleep, Father Christmas flies in on his reindeer-drawn sleigh from the North Pole to leave a few presents.

Christmas Day is family time. Everyone sits down together for a big Christmas lunch of roast turkey with all the fixins', plum pudding, and mince pie. The highlight of the festivities is the Christmas cracker. Just as in Victorian times, kids break open these wrapped paper tubes, and crack! Toys, candy, and surprises spill out. At 3:00 P.M., many families gather around the telly to watch the Queen's annual Christmas message.

Each Christmas at Somerset House, once a grand palace, the courtyard is transformed into an ice skating rink elegant enough to make a commoner feel like royalty.

London offers Christmas fun fit for a queen and streets filled with holiday cheer. When the weather doesn't cooperate, snow is trucked in to turn Trafalgar Square into a frosty wonderland.

On December 26th, Boxing Day, they "box up" gifts and tips for the servants and deliverymen (milkman and paperboy). Employers give out Christmas bonuses to workers. And, as in America, there's that time-honored tradition of department store clearance sales and merchandise returns!

We've seen how Christmas customs in England have evolved over the millennia since pre-Christian times, from venerated evergreens to . . . venerated evergreens. The tall fir tree that stands in the center of London on Trafalgar Square every Christmas is an annual gift from the Norwegians. And that's our next stop, a northern land as close to Santa's traditional home as you can get in Europe.

Londoners weary of the season's hustle and bustle stop to relax at evening Christmas concerts in the city's many acoustically—and historically—superb venues, such as St. James' Church, designed by Christopher Wren and consecrated in 1684.

NORWAY

Gledelig Jul!

A FESTIVAL OF LIGHTS

I'M IN OSLO, and it's the perfect winter scene—a full moon arcs high overhead, ice-white holiday lights sparkle in the darkness . . . and it's the middle of the afternoon! Norway, with its northern location, has the longest and darkest winters in Europe. It's also about the least church-going country in Europe. Maybe that explains why Christmas in Norway feels less like a celebration of Jesus than a pagan midwinter-fest celebrating light.

In fact, the Norwegian word for Christmas—Jul (Yule)—literally means "wheel," referring to the sun as it turns toward spring. Jul is also the name of a pre-Christian

During the dark days of the long Norwegian winter, any kind of light brings a smile to your face.

Viking drinking festival. Only in the 10th century did King Haakon I move the heathen custom of drinking Jul on the winter solstice to December 25th to celebrate the birth of Jesus. Gradually the pagan feast was Christianized.

Imagine the raucous time as medieval Norwegians celebrated the ebb of winter. Carnivores were in hog heaven, enjoying an abundance of good, fresh meat. Jul was the time when animals were slaughtered—which made more sense in that subsistence economy than feeding them through the winter.

When the beer was brewed, the animals slaughtered, and the bread baked, the house was cleaned and the party began. Santa Lucia Day (December 13th) kicked off a period when gnomes and trolls ran wild and no work was allowed. People brought in enough wood to last the entire holiday. They gave the remaining animals a little

A Norwegian pub sports Christmas trees.

extra hay and even lashed bundles of grain to posts outside their homes to feed the birds.

After a big feast, the remaining food was not cleaned up. It was left out overnight for the little people. If you neglected your *nisse*—those mischievous elves of the forest—ill fortune would hit your family.

On Christmas Day after church, *Julebukk* (caroling) groups sang and entertained door to door in exchange for goodies. In some places today, people still use horse and sleigh, and sleigh bells are often heard as folks make their way to their neighbors' for Christmas cakes and delicacies. In this season of games and merriment, nobody mentions children's bedtimes.

Today, the Norwegian Christmas season feels very low key. Commercialism has crept in, further discrediting it to secular Norwegians. Still, churches enjoy their

The land of the midnight sun is also the land of the midday moon. During Christmas season, darkness settles on Oslo by late afternoon.

best attendance of the year and are busy with Advent concerts through the season. But while Christmas concerts end with a spirited Norwegian version of *Beautiful Savior* (in which the entire audience sings the last verse together), you see almost no Christian elements in the holiday decorations. I didn't see a manger scene anywhere in my travels here. It's almost as if Christmas, timed centuries ago to coincide with the pagan solstice celebration, has reverted back to its pre-Christian roots.

Christmas in Norway is a festival of light, seeming to promise longer days and the return of the sun. Norwegians miss the sun intensely, and they need a spirit boost during those weeks when noon feels like twilight and it's dark by 4:00.

Do whatever's necessary to be on good terms with Norway's elves at Christmas time.

In good, understated Norwegian fashion, houses are decorated only with white lights—never colored—in the windows. You'll see some traditional candles, but electric lights posing as candles are more common. A plastic Santa or manger scene on the lawn, or garish colored lights along the eaves would probably put you in the neighborhood doghouse. It makes sense in a land that seems to have organized itself beyond a need for God. And this obsession with light stretches throughout the year; more than any other Europeans, Norwegians work diligently on their summer tans.

SANTA LUCIA DAY, DECEMBER 13TH

A high-"light" of the season is December 13th, the feast day of Santa Lucia, the Queen of Lights. The 13th was traditionally considered the longest night of the

year. (Actually, the solstice on the 21st is the longest night, but the 13th is the day when the sun sets earliest.) Lucia, whose name means "light," symbolizes hope and emergence out of the darkness.

Lucia, The Queen of Light, was a fourth-century Sicilian saint who (legend says) helped persecuted Christians hiding in tunnels, wearing a wreath with candles to light the way. Martyred by the Romans, she became the patron saint for the "light of the body"—the eyes.

In Norway, the legend grew from then on that in the early hours of the morning of December 13th, a young woman born of rich and noble parents—dressed in a white gown with a red sash, wearing a crown of lingonberry twigs and blazing candles—

On Santa Lucia Day, little Norwegians brighten the days of senior citizens with baskets of freshly-baked saffron buns.

went from one farm to the next. She carried a torch to light her way, bringing baked goods to each house, returning home by sunrise.

Because Lucia's name means light, many of the light-and-fire customs of the ancient Yuletide ceremonies became associated with her day. People lit "Lucy candles" in their homes and "Lucy fires" outdoors. They threw incense into the bonfires, and as the flames rose, trumpets and flutes played to celebrate the changing of the sun's course. Before the Reformation brought an increase in Christian symbolism, Santa Lucia Day in Norway (and Sweden) was one of the biggest festivals, announcing to the demons of winter that their reign would be broken, that the sun would return again, and the days would become longer.

On December 13th, churches are packed all over Norway as choirs sing Santa Lucia. *At the end of the service, the girls exit, spreading light through the village.*

Legend has it that no work should be done on the night of the holiday, Lussinatten, or else Lussi, a feared enchantress, will punish you. From then until Christmas, spirits, gnomes, and trolls roam the earth. Farmers give extra feed to farm animals, who are reputed to talk to each other on Lussinatten.

Today, Santa Lucia Day is celebrated in family gatherings, churches, schools, day-care centers, nursing homes, and hospitals. In comes a procession of girls, led by a young girl dressed as Saint Lucy (the Lussibrud, or Lucy bride), with a white robe, a crown of lights on her head, and a candle in her hand. The girls carry baskets of saffron buns *(Lussekattor)* to hand out. They're delicious with steaming coffee.

If the ceremony is in a village church, the finale of the service is not *Silent Night* but *Santa Lucia*—the same song popular in Italy but with Norwegian lyrics. As they sing, the children's choir with their leader wearing her crown of candles proceeds down the aisle and into the night, as if to spread light to the needy community.

JULENISSE: NICE OR NOT?

While Santa Claus comes from America and St. Nicholas comes from Germany, the Julenisse comes from the Norwegian forest—just behind the family barn. There are entire communities of these magical "little people" *(nisse),* who come in all shapes and sizes, but the Christmas Julenisse is a kind of cross between Father Christmas and an ordinary *nisse*. He has a red stocking cap, a long white beard, knee breeches, hand-knit stockings, a Norwegian sweater, and a homespun jacket. On top he wears a heavy fur coat—it can get cold in Norway in the winter.

The Julenisse is jolly and happy, but can also be temperamental, stern, and even a jerk. Stay on his good side by leaving a plate of cookies, or your horse might develop teeth problems, your rake will break, and your kids will wake up with rheumatism.

Old-timers believed their home's resident *nisse* was the original settler of the land. His primary duty was to protect the land and buildings, and keep the farm in good order. He was helpful so long as he got his Christmas porridge or Christmas beer and some *lefse* (potato flatbread) on Christmas Eve. Many farms would make up a bed for the *nisse* on Christmas Eve, and set an honorary place for him at the table.

Children today still grow up believing in this guy. A friend or relative dressed up as the Julenisse comes to the house with a sack of presents on Christmas. In naughty-or-nice Santa style, he asks the famous question, "Are there any good children here?" The kids put some Christmas porridge out in the barn for the Julenisse on Christmas Eve, and by golly, it's always gone the next morning.

Pamper your Julenisse, or discover what happens when elves go bad.

TREES

To the pre-Christian pagans partying their way through the dead of the Nordic winter, evergreens—swags, wreaths, and trees—promised the return of summer. Today, the dominant Norwegian Christmas icon is the evergreen tree.

The Christmas tree—usually a spruce or pine either bought in a parking lot depot (as in America) or chopped in the woods—must be fresh, green, and fragrant, to signify the idea of vitality and growth in spite of the dark winter.

The tree is strewn with tinsel, homemade ornaments, Norwegian flags, and candles that are occasionally real, but generally electric. Every mall and every town square

Even the humblest village has a tree to brighten the main square.

comes with a tall twinkling tree, capped with a star. While greenery has long decorated homes, the tradition of a decorated Christmas tree came from Germany in the 1800s. Traditionally, it's not put up and decorated until Little Christmas Eve, December 23rd. The northern European custom of the candlelit Christmas tree is derived from the belief that it sheltered woodland spirits when other trees lost their leaves during winter.

Locals love their trees. In fact, year after year, many visit the historic Bogstad Manor, perhaps the finest mansion in Oslo, to see its sumptuously decorated 19th-century-style tree. The royal family has a fondness for Christmas trees. The king's subjects knew this well when, during his World War II exile in Britain, they would smuggle a good tree to him every Christmas—cut especially for him from his cherished

A Norway spruce adorns London's Trafalgar Square each year, a gift from the people of Oslo.

homeland. The king is back in Oslo now, but each year the people of the city continue the tradition, sending a grand tree that stands on Trafalgar Square in London—a thank-you for British support during the dark years of Nazi occupation.

Norwegians enjoy holding hands around their Christmas trees and singing classic carols as they circle. You'll see bundled-up school children forming two concentric circles. Joined by a Julenisse, they move in two directions, singing as they go.

The EDIBLE SIDE of a NORWEGIAN CHRISTMAS

Christmas is a time for those once-a-year foods and drinks. Norwegians make a lot of baked goods—cookies, holiday cakes, and gingersnaps are popular. The local Christ-

mas fruitcake is called *Julekake*. The towering marzipan *kransekake* is festooned with Norwegian flags and party poppers.

Grownups enjoy hot mulled wine and a specially brewed Christmas beer, called *Juløl*. The beer is brewed on farms, a custom dating back to the pagan feast known as Joulu or Lol, when people drank from animal-horn vessels and celebrated the Norse gods Odin, Freya, and Njord. Vikings celebrated the winter solstice with this particularly stout brew. The word "Wassail" comes from a toast in Old Norse that means "To your good health." This drinking festival evolved into the tradition of visiting neighbors on Christmas Eve and drinking to their health.

The kransekake—*a tower of Christmas cheer.*

Norwegian Julekake (*Christmas Cake*)

Savor this delicious bread with lots of sweet butter slathered on top.

(Makes two loaves.)

1 cup milk
½ cup butter
2 packages active dry yeast
½ cup warm water
1 t. sugar
1 egg, lightly beaten
½ t. salt
½ cup sugar

1 t. cardamom
Approximately 5 cups sifted flour
¾ cup citron
¾ cup dried or candied cherries
¾ cup golden raisins
1 egg, for egg wash
Powdered sugar, for topping

Heat the milk and add butter to the hot milk. Cool to lukewarm.

Dissolve the yeast and 1 teaspoon sugar in warm water (100°F-110°F) and let stand for 10 minutes. Add the egg and yeast to the milk and butter mixture. Add salt, sugar, and cardamom. Beat in 2 cups of flour and mix well.

Mix the citron, cherries, and raisins together with a little flour, so the fruit doesn't stick together, and add to the mixture. Gradually add the rest of the flour, beating well after each addition, until the dough becomes pretty stiff.

Turn the dough onto a lightly floured board or cloth and knead until smooth. Place in a greased bowl. Cover and let rise until doubled in bulk. Divide the dough into two equal parts and form round loaves. Place the loaves on buttered cookie sheets and let rise until nearly double.

Preheat oven to 350°F. Brush the top of the dough with a beaten egg or egg white. Bake for 30 to 40 minutes (check for doneness by tapping lightly on the loaf; it should sound hollow). While still warm, dust the *Julekake* with powdered sugar. Decorate with candied cherries and almonds if desired.

CHRISTMAS EVE

A traditional Norwegian Christmas Eve starts at 5:00 P.M. as church bells peal, calling people—dressed up in their traditional finery—to worship. Christmas Eve is also a time when many families visit the local graveyard to pay respects to their dearly departed.

After the service, they sit down to the big family dinner that includes pickled herring salad and roast duck, goose, or pork loin. For dessert the kids are treated to a special rice porridge with an almond hidden in the mix. The child who discovers it wins a prize: a marzipan pig, a gift reminiscent of olden times, when a peasant family's

At the Christmas meal, the child who finds the almond in the porridge wins the marzipan pig.

wealth was tied up in its precious pig. Of course, a bowl of porridge is left out for the Julenisse. Many families enjoy joining hands and caroling around their tree.

After dinner, all the brooms in the house are hidden away; long ago, Norwegians believed that witches and mischievous spirits came out on Christmas Eve and stole brooms for riding.

For little children, the evening's highlight is the exciting knock on the door. A voice calls out, "Are there any good children here?" The children answer with a happy chorus of "Yes!" The door opens, and in comes the Julenisse with a sack full of gifts. The kids tear open the presents, and the family enjoys coffee and lots of special holiday cakes.

A SMALL-TOWN CHRISTMAS IN SANTA'S ZIP CODE

Norway's capital, Oslo, is the most interesting sightseeing stop in the country, though the city doesn't feel all that Christmasy. Still, the streets are decorated for the holiday, and locals not ready to rely on the Julenisse are out shopping. It is typically bare and wet; the cold only comes after Christmas these days. But wintry wonderlands are common at higher altitudes just a bit inland. The ice rink in the town center is a lively spot for people watching. The local subway zips anyone interested in some skiing or sledding into the nearby hills and up to the famous ski jump. Weekends are lively with Christmas markets, and there are lots of Christmas concerts.

Drøbak, 20 miles south of Oslo, looks like any idyllic town on a fjord. But Drøbak is famous for two things: the sinking of a Nazi warship in its narrow fjord . . . and its status as Norway's self-proclaimed capital of Christmas.

Feed the Birds

One beloved Norwegian Christmas custom begins in late autumn at harvest time. The finest wheat is gathered and saved until Christmas. This wheat is then attached to poles made from tree branches, making perches for the birds. A large circle of snow is cleared away beneath each perch. According to the legend, this provides a place for the birds to dance, allowing them to work up their appetites between meals. Just before sunset on Christmas Eve, the head of the household checks on the wheat in the yard. If a lot of sparrows are dining, it's a sign of a good year for growing crops.

In Norway, even the animals get Christmas goodies. Grain is lashed to lampposts for the birds.

Drøbak has a passion for promoting Christmas and selling the notion that it is Santa's zip code—yes, the American-style Santa Claus, who has become the Julenisse's Christmas competition. Santa's Julehus (Yule house), a converted church, overlooks the town square.

The Julehus is filled with red-clad Christmas elves, and holiday handicrafts designed by Eva Johansen and her hardworking crew. Up the street, a local restaurant serves all the traditional meals, with a fire watched over by impish elves and Julenisse. Down at the marina, the director of the tourist office grows a scraggly beard and wears his Julenisse outfit. Drøbak claims to receive 25,000 pieces of mail addressed to Santa Claus each year. They actually answer each one with a holiday greeting card, and the particularly heart-tugging letters get a small present in the mail.

Christmas in Norway is celebrated with a unique intimacy and a Scandinavian flair for community. One of my most heart-warming moments came when I enjoyed Santa Lucia Day in Drøbak's senior center, which has housed widows and seniors for over 200 years. On this day, December 13th, the kindergarteners brought us light. The kids paraded in, led by a tiny Lucia wearing her crown of lights. The children carried the traditional Santa Lucia saffron buns—a treat that brought back distant childhood memories for the adults, and kicked off lifelong memories for these kids. Endearing rituals such as these ensure that traditions stay strong from generation to generation.

FRANCE

Joyeux Noël!

As it is in so many places, Christmas in France is all about the three Fs: family, friends, and food. It's a surprisingly low-key affair, marked by family gatherings, treats for the children, and the grand, culinary high point of the year, Le Reveillon de Noël, the Christmas Eve dinner.

St. NICHOLAS and PÈRE NOËL

Though the big Christmas event in France is on Christmas Eve, the season officially starts on December 6th with a visit from St. Nicholas. According to legend, St. Nicholas arrives with a little donkey carrying baskets filled with treats. This tradition

A quiet French village awaits the arrival of Christmas.

is still re-enacted in some villages today. St. Nicholas, known as the protector of children, earned his kind reputation in France. In a particularly gruesome legend, a twisted butcher lured three French children who'd wandered off one day into a shop, where he salted them alive and stuffed them in a barrel. Happily, the children were later found and revived by good ol' St. Nick. The wicked butcher became known as Père Fouettard, and to this day he follows St. Nicholas around, a nasty character carrying a switch and threatening children.

St. Nicholas' modern counterpart is Père Noël, a slimmer version of Santa Claus, who dresses fashionably, in a long red robe trimmed in white fur. While St. Nicholas has been around since the Middle Ages, Père Noël was introduced in the early 1900s by department-store merchants in Paris who were anxious to bump up sales during the holiday season.

Sweet St. Nicks tempt chocolate lovers.

CHRISTMAS CRÈCHE

A week before Christmas, families all over France get down boxes carefully saved from Christmases past, and unwrap the *santons*, little clay figurines that represent the people of a typical village. The Doctor, the Baker, the Mayor, and others are lovingly arranged on a table or mantel, around a stable with the Holy Family. Some families add a figure each day to the circle adoring the Christ child. Children complete the Nativity scene, or crèche, with twigs and moss they find in the garden. In many homes, it's this crèche, and not the Christmas tree, that is the focus of the Christmas celebration. For two centuries, towns have hosted special fairs where locals go to buy the *santons* that will populate their manger scenes with authentic French folk characters.

Clay cattle populate a manger scene, the centerpiece of many French homes.

SAPINS DE NOËL

The French Christmas tree *(sapin)* is presumed to have its origins in medieval times, though the first on record was in the French city of Strasbourg in 1605. This big fir in the town square was decorated with paper roses, apples, and painted communion wafers, and symbolized the tree in the Garden of Eden.

In French homes these days, families set up their Christmas tree a few days before December 25th, and decorate it with homemade ornaments, candles, lights, tinsel, and colored stars. On Christmas morning, parents will often add little toys, candies, and fruits to the branches of the tree to surprise and delight their children.

With a little help from Dad—voilà! C'est magnifique!

In Paris, the Ministry of Parks and Gardens provides the city with 1,000 fir trees each Christmas season. About 300 of these firs ring the big roundabout intersection on the Champs-Elysées, where they're decorated with tiny white fairy lights. In the region of Burgundy in southeast France, people who live along country roads set out decorated evergreen trees in front of their homes. These festive evergreens cheerfully greet all those lucky enough to find themselves passing through the Burgundian countryside at Christmas.

In Paris, hundreds of lighted trees sparkle on the Champs-Elysées.

BURGUNDY:
FRANCE'S RELIGIOUS HEART

Burgundy is the quiet, religious heart of a mostly secular nation. France's venerable abbeys are located here, and their spirit seems to animate the villages in the region. A sense of community runs strong in rural France, often expressed in simple rituals shared by families and friends.

In small-town Burgundy, churches bustle with activity. Every pew is packed as families turn out to see their little ones sing carols and perform *The First Noel*. The church

A wide-eyed boy celebrates Christmas in Burgundy.

Monks, Abbeys, and Medieval Music

Le Bussière Abbey was founded in the 13th century by Cistercian monks. After the fall of the Roman Empire (A.D. 500), monasteries rose as refuges of peace and order in a chaotic world. During the Middle Ages (500–1500), industrious monks transformed this region by clearing the forest, cultivating the land, and planting a variety of crops, including grapes. Their labor is reflected in the landscape and the artisan products that Burgundy is famous for today.

A unique form of chant was developed between the 12th and 14th centuries. The Cistercian abbeys of France are renowned for their ethereal acoustics, and the austere monophonic and polyphonic music that echoes off stone walls and resonates in silent spaces is still sung there.

twinkles in candlelight, while neighbors exchange greetings and light one another's candles in a joyous communal celebration.

L^E REVEILLON DE NOËL: WAKE UP AND SMELL THE OYSTERS

In France, food is at the center of life, even in the dead of winter. The most anticipated culinary event of the year is Le Reveillon de Noël, the Christmas Eve feast. "Reveillon" literally means an "awakening." In a symbolic sense, the Reveillon is a kind of spiritual wake-up call or bugler's reveille—awakening people to the meaning of Jesus' birth.

Let's hear it for the chef!

Traditionally, the Reveillon was served after the Midnight Mass. In Paris, where people often go out with friends to celebrate, some restaurants and cafés stay open all night. But in the country, where the Reveillon is prepared and served at home, most families forego the Midnight Mass, choosing instead to celebrate with the kids.

Like most French dinners, the Reveillon is a multi-course affair lasting several hours, including appetizers, an entrée, dessert, and a cheese plate, all paired with various wines. Each region of France proudly serves its own special dishes for this feast, using local ingredients and cuisine. In Paris, the meal kicks off with raw oysters. Another popular appetizer throughout France—and a specialty of Alsace—is foie gras. French for "fat liver," the name refers to the fattened liver of a goose or duck, which is marinated in cognac or sauternes, then baked in a clay terrine dish (see

Families with young children start the Reveillon early.

page 118). In Brittany, locals enjoy buckwheat cakes and sour cream. In Provence, the people enjoy a special Christmas bread; after giving half of it to a poor person, they eat the rest.

The main course is usually a roast goose or turkey. In Burgundy, where white Charolais cattle are raised, they often serve filet of beef with locally harvested truffles, all wrapped up in buttery brioche and baked until golden (see page 120).

OYSTERS

Although the French indulge in oysters throughout the year, they're most popular at Christmastime, when 70 percent of the country's annual total is consumed. Usually

In Paris, oysters are an integral part of holiday feasting.

this means raw oysters, arranged seductively on the half-shell. For many Parisians, Christmas simply wouldn't be Christmas without oysters.

The Reveillon meal starts with an appetizer of dozens of fresh, briny oysters (different regions serve slightly different species), sometimes accompanied by small fried sausages.

Trying to pick a wine to drink with these salty-sweet wonders? A white Graves or a crisp white from the Loire Valley accompany the Fines de Claire or Arcachon oysters. A white Burgundy or Chablis premier cru goes well with the Belons. The oysters from Bouziques can match up to a strong white, such as a good muscadet. Too complicated? Pop a bottle of champagne and you can't go wrong.

In France, many believe that raw oysters enhance your appetite for . . . Christmas.

What to Pack for a Rustic Winter Picnic in Burgundy

Pastis, an aniseed apéritif, best mixed with water

Several bottles of **Beaujolais** or **Pinot Noir**

Stinky **cheeses**

Rustic **salamis**

Crunchy **baguettes**

Bacon: Bring along a small grill and sizzle over the coals.

Duck: Douse generously with red wine and roast in the fire.

More **local red wine,** for the duck, of course

Potatoes: Just toss on coals.

Potato chips, pronounced "cheeps"

Homemade Foie Gras

Prepare eight days ahead.

600–700 gram block of grade-A pure goose liver
Kosher salt
Pepper
1 clay or porcelain terrine with cover
Tweezers

Delicious foie gras goes great with a not-too-chilled white Burgundy.

In a bowl, marinate the liver in milk with ice cubes overnight.

The next day, dry the liver in a towel, then spread it out. Cut the liver in two parts lengthwise and use tweezers to remove the main vein and as many of the smaller ones as possible. Add kosher salt and a generous quantity of pepper from a pepper mill. Wrap the seasoned liver in a towel. While grasping the two ends of the towel firmly, shake for 10 minutes so that the salt and pepper impregnate the liver.

Heat the oven to 215°F and prepare a dish for a *bain-marie* (water bath). Squeeze the liver into the terrine dish and work it so that it's against the sides of the pot. Cover the terrine with lid and put in water bath. (To create a water bath, place a folded kitchen towel in the bottom of a roasting pan. Put the sealed terrine on the towel and add hot water to fill the roasting pan halfway.) Put the terrine, resting in the water bath, in the oven for one hour. Remove foie gras from the oven and let cool to room temperature, then place in fridge for eight hours.

On the day you wish to serve it, take the foie gras out of the terrine by putting the dish in warm water and running a knife around the edges. Cut fine slices with a knife rinsed in hot water after each slice. Serve with slices of toasted baguette.

Filet of Beef Tenderloin in Brioche with Truffles

Wild mushrooms can be substituted for the truffles.

Brioche:

2 t. active yeast
   (not rapid rise)

¼ cup warm milk
   (120°F to 130°F),
   plus more milk if needed

2 ½ cups all-purpose flour

½ t. kosher salt

3 eggs

Beef tenderloin:

3 to 3 ½ lbs. filet of beef tenderloin
   (filet mignon)

2 T. butter (for sautéing mushrooms and
   browning meat)

3 T. Dijon mustard

Kosher salt and freshly ground pepper

¾ to 1 cup truffles, coarsely chopped (or
   substitute a mix of chopped wild mushrooms:
   chanterelles, morels, and shitakes)

1 large egg, lightly beaten

Salt and pepper to taste

Start by making the dough. Pour the warm milk into a small bowl and sprinkle the yeast over it; mix. Stir in ¼ cup flour and mix until a soft dough forms, adding more milk if necessary. Place in a large lightly-buttered bowl, cover with a towel, and let rise in a warm place for about 30 minutes.

Using a mixer with a dough hook, place the butter and salt into a large mixing bowl and beat until soft and light. (To mix the dough by hand, use a large wooden spoon.) Add one egg and beat until smooth, then add a third of the remaining flour and mix. Beat in another egg, then another third of the flour. Finally beat in the remaining egg and the rest of the flour. Add the yeast mixture and mix thoroughly.

Knead the dough by repeatedly folding the ends to the center, rolling and turning and stretching the dough until it is supple and shiny, about 5 minutes. Place in a large lightly-buttered bowl, cover with a towel, and let rise in a warm place for at least 1 hour.

Melt 1 T. of butter in a large skillet and sauté the mushrooms until they have released their liquid. Set aside. In the same skillet, melt another 1 T. of butter and brown the beef for 5 minutes on each side. Pat the meat dry with a dish towel. Brush the beef with the mustard and sprinkle generously with salt and pepper. Cover the meat with the truffles.

Preheat oven to 350°F. Roll, stretch, and spread the dough on a large, flat surface. Place the prepared beef in the center of the dough. Wrap the dough around the meat, covering it completely and pinching the seams closed. Brush the dough with a beaten egg so that it will brown while baking. Use a knife to cut three short slits in the top to allow steam to exit. Bake for 50 minutes, or until golden brown. Let stand uncovered 10 minutes before slicing. Serve with a French pinot noir.

FOR DESSERT: AN EDIBLE LOG

The Reveillon dinner builds to the dessert, a cake called Buche de Noël (Yule Log) that recalls some of France's earliest Yuletide traditions. Back in the 12th century, the Buche de Noël was an actual, very large, freshly-cut tree. The men of the house carried the log into the home, circled the room with it three times, then laid it on the hearth. The family poured wine, oil, and salt over the log while offering prayers and singing Christmas songs. Then the mother or daughters would set the log ablaze, using a splinter saved from the previous year's Yule log.

By the 19th century, as cast-iron stoves replaced large kitchen fireplaces and hearths, the Yule log was downsized. Then the Buche became a small log that wasn't burned, just placed ceremonially on the dining table and decorated with candles and greenery.

For dessert, there's Buche de Noël, a cake topped with meringue "mushrooms" to look like a Yule log dragged out of the woods.

Today, the Buche de Noël is a Christmas cake, served on Christmas Eve. It's often made of a rolled sponge cake, filled with a silky chocolate or chestnut buttercream, and covered in chocolate-buttercream "bark," with cocoa-dusted meringue "mushrooms" and almond-paste "holly leaves," all showered with a sprinkle of confectioners'-sugar "snow."

The REVEILLON'S LAST COURSE: STINKY CHEESE

No Reveillon would be complete without stinky cheese.

Stinky cheese is odiferous. It really does stink. But it doesn't taste stinky; it tastes

Ah, the sights, sounds . . . and smells of Christmas.

robust, creamy, and sublime. Stinky cheese is made from cow's milk. Goat and sheep cheeses are tangy and strong, but they're different from ripe, cow's milk cheese that oozes stinky perfection.

Why does stinky cheese stink? Because of the bacteria that forms as the cheese matures, a mold that generates a particularly strong smell. In Burgundy, the cheese is often "washed" in a local wine or a rough brandy, which adds more complexity to the taste.

In the U.S., cheese makers are required to pasteurize cheese by heating the milk to a high temperature. Pasteurization kills potential bacteria . . . but it also kills flavor. American cheese is not very stinky. In France, pasteurization is not a requirement, so the milk is heated at lower temperatures, preserving its character.

Always bring stinky cheese to room temperature before serving. To quickly ripen, wrap in wax paper and store at room temperature. Phew! Stinky cheese is delicious with a nutty bread, but a fresh, crunchy baguette is perfectly acceptable. Hold your nose, take a bite, and . . . aaaahhh.

To make a cheese plate acceptable to French connoisseurs, it must include at least one stinky cheese and several other kinds with contrasting flavor and texture. Try these imports for an (almost) authentic French cheese plate: Epoisses (stinky), brie (creamy, subtle, nutty flavor), chabichou du Poitou (delicate, slightly acidic goat cheese), comte (hard, fruity, or nutty flavor), fourme d'Ambert (creamy with faint hints of blue mold), and Reblochon (velvety in texture, with nuts and herbs).

C'est cheese!

CHRISTMAS EVE: WAITING FOR PÈRE NOËL

Hours after the Reveillon begins, dozy uncles retire to armchairs while mothers round up eager and exhausted children for the last of the Christmas Eve rituals. In many homes, pajama-clad kids gather around the Christmas tree to sing a song or recite a poem for the family, reminding listeners of the meaning of Christmas.

Just before bed, children all over France put their slippers by the fireplace or underneath the tree in hopes that Père Noël will have filled them with small gifts in the morning. In Burgundy, the children tuck an orange and a star-shaped cookie in their slippers to thank Père Noël in advance for his kind generosity. The last thing the

Rather than a stocking by the chimney, French kids leave slippers out with a little treat for Père Noël.

children do before closing their eyes is go to the window to look for the "shepherd star" and light small candles, which they place on the windowsill to light the night while the sleeping world awaits the Nativity.

CHRISTMAS IN PARIS

Christmas in Paris is rather subtle. It's hard to make this luminous city any better with a few more lights. The best way to appreciate Paris at Christmas—or any time of year—is on foot. You never know what you might discover when you're out walking. The streets yield unexpected surprises—turn a corner and you might find yourself at an elegant arcade twinkling with red lights, or happen upon a couple of young Père Noëls belting out a duet in front of the Opera House.

Paris' Village Royale dresses up tastefully in red for Christmas.

France's glorious cathedrals, such as Notre-Dame, pack them in for Midnight Mass on Christmas Eve. Midnight Mass is an old and sacred tradition in this country, and for some people, the only church service of the year. The cathedrals, lit with countless candles, echo with the sounds of carols and hymns.

Parisian shoppers buy fewer gifts at Christmas than their American counterparts, instead favoring the small specialty shops that abound in this world capital. There are whole shops dedicated to foie gras, a traditional French Christmas gift. Chocolate shops and pâtisseries, which are wonderful at any time of the year, get even more enticing at Christmas. It's easy to spot local favorites by the lines that spill out the door.

The streets are dotted with stalls selling all sorts of scrumptious food, steamy crêpes and delicious *pain d'épice,* a spiced honey bread made only at Christmas. Follow the voices of vendors calling out, *"Chaud des marrons!"* —"Chestnuts, get 'em while they're hot!"

Shoppers with visions of Versace dancing in their heads are never far from a designer boutique, and the shops' chic seasonal windows are themselves worth the walk.

Say Merry Christmas in French: Chocolate!

Say Merry Christmas in French: Foie gras!

How to Roast a Chestnut

To make 1 pound of roasted chestnuts, start with 1 ½ pounds of chestnuts in the shell. With a sharp knife, cut an X on the flat side of each chestnut shell. Put chestnuts in a large bowl and submerge in water. Soak for at least 30 minutes, up to an hour. Drain and pat dry. Heat oven to 425°F. Place chestnuts in a single layer in a large pan. Roast uncovered for 20 minutes or until shells begin to curl up at the X. Peel chestnuts while they are warm.

Say Merry Christmas in French: Chaud des marrons!

When you've had enough, trot over to a neighborhood brasserie, grab a seat, and slurp a few of the season's best oysters alongside happy locals. *C'est la vie!*

ELEGANT EDIBLES À LA PARIS: CHOCOLATE

Is there a more perfect Christmas gift than chocolate? Is there a better place to buy it than Paris? *Mais non!*

Reputed to be the Viagra of its day, it's said that the Aztec ruler Montezuma drank vast quantities of chocolate each day before visiting his harem. And although cacao had been called "Food of the Gods" and was an important part of Central American culture for centuries, chocolate wasn't brought to the French court until 1615, when

The French celebrate Christmas (and anything else) with fine chocolate.

Louis XIII married the chocolate-drinking Anne of Austria, the Spanish Infanta. Since obtaining drinkable chocolate involved countless hours of laborious drying, grinding, and mixing, it remained a royal luxury for many years. Not until 1828, when Conrad Van Houten of the Netherlands developed a mechanical extraction method, was chocolate suddenly transformed from a rare splurge into a daily, inexpensive snack.

Today, many chocoholics view Paris as the center of the universe. No other city can claim as many world-class artisan chocolatiers as Paris can. The city's chocolate is high art and très chic. Handmade from superlative ingredients, Parisian chocolates include the finest cacao and unique flavorings, ranging from lavender to caramel to Earl Grey tea. From the richly thick hot chocolate at Chez Angelina to the jewel-like morsels at La Maison du Chocolat, Parisian chocolatiers bring the delicacy to heights unimagined by the early Aztecs.

Two French Christmas treats in one: chestnuts . . . made of chocolate.

EPIPHANY CAKES,
OR GALETTE DES ROIS

All over France, the Epiphany season is celebrated by eating Galette des Rois, or Cake of Kings. For several days before Christmas until January 6, when the Feast of Epiphany occurs, the French line up to buy *galette* after *galette* in *pâtisseries* and *boulangeries* for dinner parties, snacks, and mid-afternoon teas.

The reason for this enormous amount of pastry consumption? Each *galette* hides a trinket, usually a tiny porcelain figurine, ranging from Harry Potter or Zorro to miniature paintings of *Guernica* or *Mona Lisa*. They're called *fèves*, after the fava beans that were the original trinkets. Each one is highly collectible. Along with the *fèves*, every *galette* is topped by a colorful paper crown. Traditionally, the *galette* is cut while the youngest child at the table designates who will get each piece, so there's no cheating. Everyone takes careful bites of the pastry until someone excitedly finds the *fève*. The winner gets the crown as well as the trinket, and becomes king or queen for the day.

The tradition dates back to the 14th century. Supposedly, the cardinals of Besançon held a lottery on the Epiphany to choose a new chapter head. Whoever got the coin hidden in the loaf of bread was the winner. Gradually the coin became a bean and the bread a *galette*. In the 1960s, the *fève* evolved into a figurine.

In the north of France, *galettes* are round puff-pastry cakes, usually filled with almond frangipane. In Brittany, *galettes* resemble a shortcake and are made with world-famous Breton butter. And in the south of France, *galettes* are brioche decorated with candied fruit and flavored with brandy or orange-flower water. Although they differ in both flavor and appearance, all Galettes des Rois contain those much-coveted *fèves* and a golden paper crown, allowing you to attain royalty for a day.

TOP TEN THINGS
TO DO IN PARIS AT CHRISTMAS

I. MANEGES DE NOEL: CHRISTMAS CAROUSELS

These seasonal merry-go-rounds pop up in every neighborhood in Paris. The biggies are at Hôtel de Ville and the Eiffel Tower, but more fun are the charming *maneges* in less touristy neighborhoods.

Spinning in the season in front of Paris' City Hall.

2. Lick a Window

The French phrase for window shopping is *lèche-vitrine*, literally, "window licking." Big department stores compete with one another for the most fabulous window displays of animation and whimsy. French parents dress up their kids and come from all over the country to compare the windows of the four great Parisian department stores: Galeries Lafayette, Printemps, Bon Marché, and Samaritaine. Thoughtfully, the stores provide wooden steps at the windows so that even the tiniest tot can get a good view.

Parisian window-shopping stokes a child's Christmas fantasies.

3. SLURP AN OYSTER IN THE MARAIS

To eat an oyster in public: Make sure to cut under the oyster so that it is completely separated from the shell. Then tip the shell towards your mouth, causing the oyster to slide forward and down into your mouth—but whatever you do, don't let any stray oyster juice run down your chin. Slurp!

4. PONY RIDES

Take the little people to Luxembourg Garden to ride the ponies or (sometimes at Christmas) donkeys. If you're lucky enough to be there when the donkeys are, tell the kids about pregnant Mary and Joseph riding the donkey to Bethlehem.

A pony ride in the park with the dome of the Panthéon rising in the distance.

5. Chocolate Shopping

Buy your best friend a box of chocolates from one of La Maison du Chocolat boutiques, run by Robert Linxe, the high priest of Paris chocolate. Specialties include jewel-like bonbons with lemon, mint, and ginger-infused fillings. The lines go out the door at Christmastime, so allow plenty of time for your visit. La Maison du Chocolat has five boutiques in Paris:

225 rue du Faubourg St-Honore, 75008 Paris
52 rue Francois 1er, 75008 Paris
8 boulevard del la Madeleine, 75009 Paris
19 rue de Sevres, 75006 Paris
89 avenue Raymond Poincare, 75016 Paris

Chocolate! Always worth the wait.

6. Avante-Garde Trees

Visit the annual exhibition of Christmas trees created by top couturiers and designers at the Pompidou Center. The "trees" don't look much like your standard evergreen, they're Christmas concoctions with something vaguely tree-like about them. Creations are by turns wickedly funny, seductive, political, lovely, and just plain weird. It's a fun exhibit and your entrance fee goes to a French charity that assists orphaned children.

A modern Christmas tree is all dressed up and ready to step out on the town.

7. THE CHAMPS-ELYSEES AND THE EIFFEL TOWER

Bundle up, wander over to the Champs-Elysées and walk the length of the boulevard with its fairy forest of twinkling trees. Time it so that you can walk (or take the Métro) over to Trocadero square in time to see the lights on the Eiffel Tower shimmer—on the hour for 10 minutes every night until midnight.

Europe's grandest boulevard, the Champs-Elysées, is at its grandest each Christmas.

8. PASTRIES, PASTRIES, PASTRIES

Indulge yourself with a Buche de Noel from the oldest pâtisserie in Paris. One day in 1730, Queen Mary Lescynska, daughter of the king of Poland, stopped in Strasbourg on her way to Versailles to marry Louis XV and met a pastry chef named Störher. She fell in love—not with the chef—but with his famous *puit d'amour* ("wells of love," chocolate cups filled with a rich, creamy custard). The Queen offered him a job, Störher packed up, opened up a pâtisserie in Paris and became famous. Even the Queen of England couldn't resist a stop at Ströher's on her last trip to Paris. (It's at 52 rue Montorgueil, 75002 Paris.)

. . . and still more pastries.

9. The City of Light's Lights

Walk up and down the Boulevard Haussmann admiring the fabulous lights at Printemps and Galeries Lafayette. It takes 150,000 bulbs to create Galeries Lafayette's illuminated canvas.

10. Ice Skating at 200 Feet

Put on something chic and cozy. Then ride the elevator to the first level of the Eiffel Tower to glide on Paris' highest ice-skating rink and gaze at the city's domes, towers, and rooftops—The City of Light illuminated for the holiday season (see photo at right).

Paris' grand department stores turn on all their lights for the holidays, simulating the stained glass of a Gothic cathedral.

Ice-skating halfway up the Ice-ful Tower

GERMANY
Fröhliche Weihnachten!

THE CRADLE of CHRISTMAS

GERMANY IS WHERE many of today's signature Christmas traditions were born—the decorated Christmas tree, enduring carols (such as *O Tannenbaum*), nutcrackers, gingerbread cookies, and the legend of St. Nicholas. Germans celebrate for an entire month, beginning at Advent. Many cities close off their main square to everyday traffic and host *Christkindlesmarkts*—Christmas markets—where shoppers come to browse for that perfect gift or Christmas ornament. The most famous of these markets is in the heartland of German Christmas, the Bavarian city of Nürnberg (Nuremberg). Here you'll savor classic holiday themes—glittering trees, old-time carols, sparkling lights, and good food and drink.

In Germany, even the wooden toys sing the praises of Christmas.

NÜRNBERG'S CHRISTMAS MARKET

Cradling a cup of hot-spiced wine as a hand warmer, I strolled through Nürnberg's main square in the shadow of the church steeple and took it all in. Over 200 wooden stalls housed local artisans dealing in all things Christmas. It was a festive swirl of heartwarming holiday sights, sounds, and scents. Bundled-up shoppers and kids sampled fresh gingerbread, rode the carousel, listened to roving brass quintets, marveled at the newest toys, and crowded in for a photo with Santa.

Nürnberg, a toy-making center for centuries, has long prided itself on the quality of its market. With no canned music, fake greenery, plastic kitsch, or war toys, it feels classier than your average crafts fair. As far back as 1610, a proclamation warned that "indecent joke articles would be confiscated." Over two million visitors annually

Germany's ultimate Christmas market lights the main square in Nürnberg.

appreciate the handcrafted feel of the classic toys and ornaments. The merchants' stalls are old-style wood huts with traditional ambience, and each year the most beautiful stall is awarded the prestigious "Prune Man" trophy.

PRUNE PEOPLE, NUTCRACKERS, SMOKING POSTMEN, AND GOLDEN ANGELS

Nürnberg's most famous toy is a homemade figurine made of fruit. Over a wire frame, it has a walnut head, four-fig body, and prune limbs, all dolled up in a Bavarian folk costume. According to legend, a Nürnberg man was on his death bed, but local

Wire together dried figs, prunes, and a walnut, paint and dress to taste, and you have a Prune Man.

schoolchildren sang him back to health. In gratitude, he gathered what he had in the house—wire, figs, prunes, and walnuts—and made them a little man as a thank-you gift. It was such a hit that later he sold more in a stall like the ones filling the market square today. They became a popular Christmas decoration and a cottage industry in Nürnberg.

All of Germany's holiday markets are a Christmasy fantasy of tiny figurines. Nutcrackers, strong-jawed to crack even the toughest nuts, are usually authority figures like soldiers, policemen, and constables. "Smokers," which are small carvings of woodworkers, loggers, postmen, and other common folk, send out fragrant incense from their tiny smoke-ring-blowing mouths.

Many of these classic wooden figurines originated in the highly forested region of

Saxony in eastern Germany. When the iron ore and silver mines went out of business back in the 15th century, Saxon miners became woodworkers.

A popular Nürnberg decoration is the candle chime. A multi-tiered wooden stand holds candles, which heat a pinwheel on top, causing it to spin. Each level of the stand features a different carved scene—a Nativity, forest critters, nutcrackers, or miners at work. It's said these chimes were especially popular in mining communities because of the miners' hunger for, and appreciation of, light.

The golden Rausch Angel hovering above the market is an icon of Christmas in Nürnberg. The name is a bit of German onomatopoeia—*rausch* is the sound of wind blowing through the angel's gold foil wings. For locals, there's no better way to cap your home's Christmas tree than with a miniature version of this angel.

Nürnberg's Rausch Angels still rustle in the wind.

A TASTE OF CHRISTMAS

Nürnberg's Christkindlesmarkt thrives into the evening as shoppers enjoy some old-time fast food. Spicy smoke billows from stalls selling the famous Nürnberg bratwurst, skinny as your little finger. Stick three of them on a crunchy fresh roll, then add a generous squirt of spicy mustard.

At the next stall, wrap your mittens around a mug of hot-spiced wine. A disposable paper or plastic cup would ruin the experience, so you must pay a deposit for a nicely decorated ceramic one. Either return the mug or keep it as a collectible, since each year there's a different model.

The famous Nürnberg bratwurst—skinny as St. Nick's little finger.

Glühwein: Christkind's Hot Spiced Wine

Germany's top poet and playwright, Goethe, wrote: "A shot of punch helps heat up the parlour." As far back as ancient Rome, wine was made hot and sweet in winter by adding honey and spices. Today, cold souls all over Germany get a seasonal lift as market square stalls sell the hot, sweet-and-spicy Glühwein. There are as many ways to prepare hot red wine punch as there are ways to decorate *O Tannenbaum*. Here's the recipe we enjoyed in Nürnberg—it's easy to make, and goes down just right as you sit around the fireplace in the Christmas season.

For a non-alcoholic version, substitute fresh apple cider instead of the wine.

(Serves 4-6)

1 bottle dry red table wine (750 ml.)
5 T. granulated sugar, or to taste
12 whole cloves, or to taste
1 cinnamon stick
Zest of 1 lemon
Freshly grated nutmeg (optional)

Combine all the ingredients in a heavy-bottomed saucepan over medium-high heat and bring to a simmer (don't let it boil). Simmer 5 minutes and strain into mugs or stemless wine glasses. For extra fragrance and spice, garnish with freshly grated nutmeg.

GINGERBREAD

Bakeries crank out traditional gingerbread—the Lebkuchen Nürnberg—using the same recipe they did in the 17th century. Back then, Nürnberg was the gingerbread capital of the world, and a stroll through the market makes it clear that the city's love affair with the cake continues.

Germany's gingerbread tradition—whether as a spiced cake, cookie, or even a small loaf—has spread throughout Europe. Some believe the name "gingerbread" comes from the Old French *gingebras*, which comes from the Latin name of the spice, *Zingebar*.

Medieval Crusaders first introduced the spices, almonds, and fruits that make up gingerbread when they returned to Europe from the Middle East. Catholic monks

Gingerbread—the heart of Christmas cooking.

popularized the treat by baking special theme cakes for saints' days and festivals. As ingredients became cheaper, gingerbreads became a popular folk sweet, and regions developed their own unique styles.

In medieval England, local bakers sold molded cookies of honey, wine, breadcrumbs, and spices. This was a cooked and thickened dough, though it wasn't baked. The cookies were cut into the commonplace shapes of daily life—men, women, the sun and moon, flowers, birds, and animals. Sometimes the dough was simply cut into round "snaps"—gingersnaps, popular today in England.

In Belgium and the Netherlands, Sinterklaas (St. Nicholas) kicked off a long month of feasting with gingerbread cookies shaped like windmills, farm animals, or farm men and women. Like the earlier medieval cakes, these were embellished with ornate surface detail, made by pressing carved cookie boards onto the rolled dough.

Characters from well-known folk tales and legends (like Hansel and Gretel) became popular gingerbread decorations.

Germany's forte has always been flat, shaped gingerbreads. At every autumn fair in the country, you'll find rows and rows of stalls filled with hundreds of gingerbread hearts, decorated with icing and tied with ribbons.

NÜRNBERG'S FAMOUS GINGERBREAD

For four centuries, the families of Nürnberg have bought their gingerbread at the thriving Christkindlesmarkt. The gingerbread was not baked in the home, but was made exclusively by a guild of master bakers, the Lebkuchler.

In Nürnberg, the gingerbread is made the old-fashioned way.

The city became known as the "Gingerbread Capital of the World," and the cake itself became a work of art. Well-known sculptors, painters, and goldsmiths added ornament and detail. Carvers whittled intricate wooden molds of hearts, angels, and wreaths. Painters frosted the cookies or added a flourish of gold paint. Gingerbread was soon sold all over Europe at fairs, carnivals, and markets.

While munching your spicy cookie, consider these morsels of history: In 1486, Emperor Friedrich III, residing in Nürnberg Castle, ordered 4,000 Lebkuchen decorated with his image. Then he invited the children of the town to gather near the castle. He greeted the children, and gave each one a gingerbread cookie. Tasty public relations! In 1855, when King Maximilien II of Bavaria visited the city, a huge gingerbread was baked in his honor. It was so big that it took four men to carry it in the welcome procession.

A Lebkuchler slides a gingerbread loaf into a traditional oven.

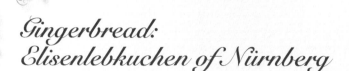

Gingerbread: Elisenlebkuchen of Nürnberg

Elisenlebkuchen are considered the finest of Germany's Christmas ginger-breads. Traditionally these Lebkuchen are baked on edible *Oblaten* (communion-like wafers), but wax paper can be substituted.

(Makes about 2 dozen cookies)

1 cup plus 2 T. sugar
4 large egg whites
¼ cup honey
3 T. apricot jam
⅓ cup marzipan
2 cups skinned hazelnuts, toasted
   and finely ground
⅓ cup candied lemon peel
⅓ cup candied orange peel
½ t. cinnamon
½ t. freshly-ground nutmeg

¼ t. ground cloves
¼ t. ground ginger
¼ t. ground cardamon
¼ t. salt
½ cup flour
1 t. baking powder
Halved almonds
1 ½ cups confectioners' sugar
1 T. water
½ t. lemon juice

In the metal bowl of an electric mixer, mix together the sugar, egg whites, honey, and jam. Place the bowl in a pan of simmering water (similar to the double-boiler method). Stirring frequently, heat the mixture until it reaches the temperature of a warm bath. Transfer the bowl back to the mixer and add the marzipan, hazelnuts, and candied lemon and orange peels.

In a separate bowl, combine the spices, salt, flour, and baking powder. Mix the dry ingredients into the egg mixture until thoroughly combined. Cover and let sit in the refrigerator overnight.

Spread the *Oblaten* on large baking sheets (or line baking sheets with wax paper). Dampen your hands and roll dough into balls, about 2 tablespoonfuls apiece. Place one on each round of *Oblaten* and flatten slightly. Press an almond half into the top of each cookie and let stand in a warm room to dry for 24 hours.

Preheat oven to 350°F. Bake 11–15 minutes or until the surface of the cookie no longer appears wet. Transfer to racks to cool.

In a large bowl, mix together the confectioners' sugar, water, and lemon juice. Brush cookies with icing and let set, about one hour.

ST NICK, CHRISTKIND, ETC.

As in much of the world, German kids pose with their local version of Santa Claus. But Germany adds a few more incarnations to the legend of Santa.

First, many Germans—especially in Catholic regions—still revere St. Nicholas on his feast day, December 6th. Like the historical St. Nicholas, a kind and generous bishop who lived in western Turkey in the fourth century, this Christmas figure arrives bearing gifts and candy for the kids.

But Germany is Luther country. In the early 1500s, the Great Reformer, Martin Luther, wanted to humanize the Christmas story, to move the focus away from saints and back to Jesus. Rather than Jolly Old St. Nicholas bringing the goodies on

German kids don't discriminate. They'll take the Christkind, St. Nicholas ... and even Santa Claus.

December 6th, Luther established the idea that gifts should be given on December 25th by the Christ child himself—"Christ child" in German is "Christkindl," or "Christkind."

But it was hard for kids to imagine the baby in the manger delivering gifts, so the tradition evolved further (though the name Christkind stuck). In Germany today, the Christkind is not the baby Jesus, but a young female angel who serves as the gift-giving Christ child. On Christmas Eve, the angel flies from house to house, leaving presents for the kiddies, tinkling a little bell as she goes.

In Nürnberg every year in late November, this angel—in the form of one lucky teenager—makes a public appearance. Dressed in white, with glittering gold wings and a golden crown, she steps out on the church balcony high above the market square

Riding the train to St. Nick's haus.

to kick off the Christmas season by opening the Christkindlesmarkt. She gazes over the square, which is laden with colorful goodies and jammed with bundled locals, and declares: "Welcome young and old—especially the young at heart—to my little community of wood and cloth. While this market's splendor is fleeting, the joy it brings is eternal." From that day until Christmas, she spends her reign spreading the spirit of the season.

CHRISTKINDMANIA

Nürnberg's Christkind, usually about 17 years old, is chosen in a city-wide contest and serves for two seasons. She has serious responsibilities. She has her own van

Nürnberg's angelic Christkind weaves sugar plum dreams for countless German children.

with chauffeur (itself a prestigious gig), and is met by paparazzi wherever she goes. With her golden crown, Goldilocks wig, white and gold outfit, genuine smile, and ethereal presence, the Christkind is understandably popular: She has over a hundred engagements in December alone. Locals brag that she even presides in the capital, Berlin, and the year after her reign in Germany she reprises her role for the German community in Chicago.

Each day she meets with countless wide-eyed children. Parents standing in the back of the room seem as enamored by their children's love of the Christkind as the children are with the sweet Teutonic angel. Even jaded TV cameramen can't stop smiling when they film the Christkind meeting her fans. You can't look at her without feeling Christmasy.

"If you're very, very gentle, you can touch my wings."

At the end of one of her appearances, Nürnberg's favorite angel allows countless kids to enjoy a Christmas fantasy. The Christkind concludes her visits by telling them, "If you're very, very gentle you can touch my wings." The star-struck children climb very, very gently onto the stage and very, very gently mob the 17-year-old superstar to touch her golden wings.

I was given an interview with her while we were filming our TV special. I had to submit my questions ahead of time, then wait in a star-strewn, generously-tinseled media room. I asked her if she would give me a peck on the cheek as a part of our mistletoe montage and she explained that wasn't allowed. But she could (and did) let me give her a peck on her angelic cheek.

"Even if you're very, very gentle, I won't kiss your cheek. But you can kiss mine."

A FAMILY CHRISTMAS EVE

Driving around Germany on December 20th, you'll see plenty of Christmas trees—but they're all still bundled up in the corner of a parking lot, waiting to be sold. No one buys a tree until just before the 25th. Traditionally, Mom and Dad decorate *O Tannenbaum* in secret and keep it hidden from the children until it's dramatically unveiled on Christmas Eve.

Though late to buy their trees, Germans decorate them with flair and delight. In fact, it was in Germany in the 1500s that the tradition of decorating trees began. Along with ornaments and lights (originally candles), they also add cookies and candies, often topping the tree with a Nürnberg Rausch Angel. Underneath it they place their

In Germany, the tree is decorated late and kept secret from the children until Christmas Eve.

Candy Canes:
Peppermint Pacifiers

The first candy canes were simple, straight white sticks of sugar candy used by Germans to decorate their Christmas trees. Then in 1670, a choirmaster at Köln Cathedral, fed up with noisy kids ruining the services, passed them out during a Living Crèche service to keep the restless children quiet. He bent the ends to depict a shepherd's crook. In the 1800s, German immigrants to America popularized the practice of using them to decorate Christmas trees. In the 1920s, the crooked white candy finally earned its stripes: An innovative American manufacturer added red stripes and mass-produced them, creating a global phenomenon.

wrapped presents, along with a brilliantly decorated plate for each family member, loaded with fruits, nuts, marzipan, chocolate, and biscuits.

For Christmas Eve, some families have a humble meal, with the big feast coming on Christmas Day. Others pull out all the stops, with a goose and dumplings, traditional veggies such as beets, and salad, followed by the ever-present gingerbread for dessert.

Then comes the big moment. The children huddle anxiously outside the living room door, waiting to go in. "Tingalingaling!" A tiny bell announces that the magical Christkind has just passed through the house. The door opens and the eager children burst into the room. There, for the first time, they see the sparkling tree and—more importantly—what the Christkind has left under it. They tear open the gifts, sing carols, light sparklers, then gather together to read the Bible story about the birth of Jesus, the original Christkind.

The Christmas goose gets everyone's full attention.

AUSTRIA

Fröhliche Weihnachten!

A MONTH OF CHRISTMAS

HENNE SITS ME DOWN and pulls out family photos of Christmas. "There's Petra," she says, "she is lighting the first candle on the Advent wreath." She pages back. "And here we all are making the wreath. For us, Advent is very important—it starts a full month of Christmas."

In predominantly Catholic Austria, the period before Christmas is a time of thoughtful preparation for celebrating the birth of Jesus. With one of Europe's shortest workweeks, Austria is known for its slow-paced, stop-and-smell-the-strudel attitude. For Christmas, Austrians start early, go slow, and touch all the holiday bases.

Lighting candles on the Advent wreath, children are taught to anticipate the birth of Jesus.

It all begins four Sundays before Christmas with Advent, the period awaiting the "arrival" of Jesus. Families make or buy an *Adventkranz*, or Advent wreath, usually made of fir or spruce. It's decorated with four candles that are lit successively on the four Sundays leading up to December 24th.

The EVIL KRAMPUS

December 5th is Krampus Day. With frightening fur, bulging eyes, and a long red tongue, Krampus runs through the streets creating chaos—banging huge cowbells and rattling chains wildly—trying to scare kids into being good. But it's all done in fun, with much teasing and laughter, and children and adults get back at the horned devil by pelting him with snowballs. Krampus' true purpose is simply to remind kids to behave well, and in this way he acts as a companion to St. Nicholas.

St. NICHOLAS in AUSTRIA

The following day, December 6th, is the feast day of St. Nicholas, the patron saint of children, who's widely honored throughout Austria. Nicholas is an "ancestor" of Santa Claus and a "relative" of Father Christmas (both celebrated on Christmas Eve and Day), but in Austria his feast day is a big deal, and separate from Christmas. With his traditional flowing robe, tall bishop's miter, and shepherd's staff, he parades through town carrying a thick book in which the good and bad deeds of the children are recorded.

Sometimes St. Nicholas is accompanied by his devilish assistant, Knecht Ruprecht (a regional version of Krampus). Knecht Ruprecht dresses in rags, with a sack over his shoulder to carry off naughty little kids. In typical good-cop/bad-cop style, Nicholas gives out sweets and apples to the good children while his companion playfully beckons "little sinners" to feel the sting of his golden rod.

AUSTRIA'S BELOVED
SILENT NIGHT: STILLE NACHTE

One of the world's best-known Christmas carols, translated into more than 250 languages, was born in small-town Austria nearly two centuries ago.

According to legend, a local priest (Joseph Mohr) went out one Christmas night to bless a newborn baby. As he walked home in the snow, he was so moved by the stillness of the starlit, holy night that he wrote a poem about it. He later gave the poem

"Stille nacht, heilige nacht..."

to Franz Gruber, his church organist, who quickly composed a tune. On Christmas Eve of 1818 the carol was sung for the first time in the village church, accompanied only by a guitar. No one could have known the impact this composition would have on the world.

The song's lullaby-like melody and simple message of heavenly peace caught on and spread. Legends from World War I tell of soldiers in opposing trenches singing *Silent Night,* mortal adversaries raising their voices in song—together but in different languages. For a short time, hatred and killing stopped, the roar of the battlefield faded, and enemies shared a holy night of "heavenly peace." Today the song can be heard from small-town street corners in mid-America to magnificent cathedrals in Europe, from outdoor candlelight concerts in Australia to palm-thatched huts in northern Peru.

Silent Night, *the most loved Christmas carol, was first sung in Oberndorf, a small town just outside of Salzburg.*

I visit the small town of Arnsdorf, Austria. In the very house where Franz Gruber lived when he composed the music, they are holding a late afternoon service that features a performance of the song. Then villagers and visitors light candles and walk in procession to nearby Oberndorf. Singing traditional carols from the region, they follow the same path through the same cold December twilight air that inspired Joseph Mohr's original poem.

In Oberndorf, they congregate at the Silent Night Chapel, which is built on the site of that first *Silent Night* performance in 1818. (The original church of St. Nicholas was torn down in the early 20th century after sustaining flood damage from the nearby Salzach River.) The Silent Night Chapel stands on the spot in front of the main altar where Gruber and Mohr stood with the choir and sang the opening lines of the timeless six-stanza carol: *"Stille Nacht, heilige Nacht...."*

Dashing through the snow, we journey in the land of Silent Night *to a traditional Tirolean Christmas.*

The original pulpit and altars from the old church were moved across town to another church. There, at Christmas Midnight Mass, singers stand in front of the same altars and recreate the moment when the song heard 'round the world was first performed.

In Austria today there are *Silent Night* museums, memorials, and markers in Salzburg, Oberndorf, Arnsdorf, Hallein, Wagrain, and a dozen more charming alpine villages with some connection to Gruber and Mohr.

The popularity of their song could almost be termed miraculous. After all, a modest curate wrote the words and a musician hardly known outside his own province composed the music. There was no celebrity to sing at the world premiere and no mass-communication systems to spread the fame of the song. However, its powerful

Austria's Silent Night *spreads the Bible's story of Jesus' birth throughout the world.*

message of heavenly peace has crossed all borders and language barriers, conquering the hearts of Christmas-celebrating people everywhere.

CHRISTMAS IN SALZBURG

Nestled under its formidable castle on a hill, Salzburg celebrates the holidays with an alpine elegance. Festive shopping lanes delight browsers. Markets are busy as locals gather last-minute holiday decorations and delicacies. It's easy to work up an appetite at the Christkindlesmarkt, with its wafting aromas of pretzels, sausage, roasted chestnuts in paper cones, and hot-spiced wine. Other booths sell Christmas candies, sweets, and cookies. Inviting cafés offer a cozy hot chocolate and strudel break. And from the castle ramparts, high above town, the roar of cannons announces the

Christmas is a blast in Salzburg.

Christmas season, the traditional gunners celebrating as they have since they really believed these shots would scare away evil.

Salzburg, nicknamed "the Rome of the north," has a magnificent cathedral, inspired by St. Peter's in Rome. The archbishop leads the service as the cathedral choir and orchestra, filling the loft in the back of the nave, perform a Christmas Mass. Locals here in the town of Mozart pack the place to mix worship with glorious music.

AN AUSTRIAN FAMILY CHRISTMAS

On December 24th, when cities can be frantic with last-minute shoppers, the country-side is a refuge for quiet traditions and simple, meaningful celebrations.

At Christmas Mass in Salzburg, the organist pulls out all the stops.

I visit the Weissacher family on their farm in Tirolea. Jakob Weissacher welcomes us with a traditional yodel, then brings us inside where his kids are busy baking cookies with grandma.

In a Christmas Eve tradition, Herr Weissacher lights incense and leads the family in a parade through the home and stables. Dad swings the smoking cauldron of incense while little Petra follows behind with a fir branch, flicking out holy water blessed by the village priest. Together, they bless the farm and pray for a happy and healthy new year.

With the home thoroughly "smoked," Jakob chalks the year and the initials of the Three Wise Men on the archway of the stable door—C for Caspar, M for Melchior, and B for Balthazar—to protect his animals from sickness in the coming year.

Traditional Austrians give their house a smoky Christmas blessing.

While Jakob keeps the kids busy, Henne sets to work secretly decorating the Christmas tree. She uses the children's homemade ornaments, plus handcrafted decorations that have been treasured for many years. Silver and gold garlands crisscross the tree, and Henne attaches real candles. Most Austrians would never dream of lighting their own trees with anything other than the traditional Christmas candles. Beneath the tree, she arranges an elaborate manger scene, with hand-carved figures handed down from generation to generation.

It's time. The kids gather anxiously, a bell rings, and the door is opened, revealing the Christmas tree, which is glistening with dozens of real candles, colored ornaments, gold and silver garlands, sparklers, candies, and cookies. This year's Weihnachtsbaum is the most magical ever!

An Austrian family enjoys cookies baked by the kids.

In traditional households like the Weissachers', children are taught restraint. Before they open the presents, they settle down with the family. Father opens the Bible and reads the story of the first Christmas. Then they all gather around the tree and sing traditional Christmas carols, with special emphasis given to *Silent Night*. In other countries, this carol may be played for weeks before Christmas, but in Austria, *Silent Night* is heard on the radio for the first time on Christmas Eve, then repeated hourly. The effect is spellbinding.

As midnight approaches, the sound of trumpets can be heard echoing across the countryside. It's the Turmblasen (tower-blowers), who climb the church steeple to call the faithful to worship with Christmas music. The adults and older children dress up for the traditional Mitternachtsmette, the Midnight High Mass. The service

"Can I open it now?" Not until Father reads from the family Bible.

commonly features music written by Franz Gruber, the composer of *Silent Night,* who also wrote nearly a hundred Masses, hymns, and carols.

In many villages, pious "shelter-seekers" spend Christmas Eve plodding through deep snow from farm to farm, re-enacting the plight of Mary and Joseph as they sought shelter on the eve of Christ's birth.

Christmas Day, December 25th, is one of quiet celebration and happy reunions with relatives and friends. It starts 12 more days of religious observance (and more work holidays!), capped by Epiphany, when the Three Wise Men visited baby Jesus. In our travels through Europe, the most vibrant celebrations of Christian traditions were in laid-back Austria.

Prosit! *And* Fröhliche Weihnachten *to all!*

ITALY

Buon Natale!

ROME IS RICH in sacred sights. For centuries, pilgrims have come from all over Christendom to the Eternal City, using the great domes and ancient obelisks as street markers to lace together the most sacred stops: catacombs, grottos, churches, fabled relics, and most important . . . the tomb of St. Peter, which for five hundred years has been marked by St. Peter's Basilica and the greatest dome on Earth. Rome is the home of Vatican City, the headquarters of the Roman Catholic Church, and the birthplace of some of Europe's most sacred Christmas traditions.

PAGAN ROOTS:
STILL CARRYING THE TORCH

Christmas in Italy is rooted in the pagan traditions of the ancient Roman Empire. The biggest event on the Roman social calendar was Saturnalia, a wild and crazy

Rome's sacred skyline

midwinter bash that went on for days. Saturnalia—a solstice-themed holiday that honored Saturn, the god of agriculture—was a hedonistic time. Toga-clad partiers paraded by torchlight through the streets, giving thanks for their crops by drinking and eating heartily. The normal Roman social order was flip-flopped and slaves and peasants became masters for a day. Pagan Martha Stewarts decorated the city with evergreen wreaths and gave beeswax candles as gifts.

The Christmas custom of hanging an evergreen wreath on the front door is borrowed from an ancient Roman New Year celebration. Romans used to wish each other good health by exchanging branches of evergreens (such as bay leaf and palm), which symbolize vitality even in the middle of winter. They called these gifts *strenae,* after Strenia, the goddess of health. It became a favored custom to bend these branches into a ring and hang them on doorways for all to enjoy.

A wreath over the door—ancient in origin—wishes good health to all who pass by.

The pagan practice of celebrating midwinter with fire continued into Christian medieval times, with Christ symbolized through fire as the Light of the World. Though these bonfire-and-torchlight processions have flickered and faded in modern times, some have survived in rural areas. In Abbadia di San Salvatore, a mountainous village near Montalcino, every Christmas Eve villagers still celebrate the Fiaccole di Natale, or Festival of Christmas Torches.

For more than a thousand years, Abbadia's faithful have gathered with shepherds (now mostly townsfolk who dress up as shepherds—see page 10), who come down from the hills to keep vigils on the Eve of Christmas. Warming themselves by the great bonfires, the faithful sing carols as they remember the lullabies that, according to legend, the shepherds sang to soothe Mary during her labor on the first Christmas.

In village Italy, traditional bonfires still warm the faithful as they honor the birth of their Lord.

Today, in the days leading up to Christmas Eve, the villagers carefully build nearly a hundred pyramids of wood, each 15 feet high, in the small streets and little squares of the village. One special person is chosen to light the first fire, which will burn with the others until dawn. When all the bonfires have been lit, townsfolk carry torches through the winding streets and sing old shepherding carols. Afterwards, everyone gathers around the bright fires to sizzle sausages and sip wine long into the night.

LA BEFANA:
THE GOOD WITCH OF CHRISTMAS

One of Italy's best-loved traditions, La Befana is a cheerful Christmas witch who brings children gifts for Epiphany, January 6th.

Rome's Christmas witch, La Befana, haunts, then delights local children.

My Roman friend, Francesca, is adamant that Italy's beloved Befana is "100% Roman," and holds a special place in her city's popular imagination. On the eve of Epiphany, the Befana flies over the rooftops of Rome on her broom and brings gifts to the good children or coal for the bad ones—although, these days the "coal" is a crunchy black confection sold at street-corner carts. According to Francesca, the children of Rome leave the Befana a snack of some soft ricotta cheese since she has hardly any teeth.

Some Roman parents threaten naughty kids with, *"Lo dico alla Befana!"* (I'll tell the Befana!), or the ever-popular, *"Viene la Befana e ti porta via!"* (The Befana will come and take you away!), which is very bad indeed, because Befana has an ogre of a husband who devours children.

According to legend, the three Wise Men stopped to ask La Befana for directions to Bethlehem and the Christ child, but she was too busy to help. As time passed,

Many Italians celebrate with Babbo Natale on Christmas and La Befana on Epiphany.

Befana kept thinking about the strange visitors and their quest. With a sack filled with bread, she set out to find baby Jesus, too. Whenever she saw a baby boy, she broke off a crust of bread and gave it to him, hoping he might be the Christ child. Befana still wanders through Italy each Christmas season looking for the baby and leaving little goodies for the children. Her name means "gift-bringer."

The legend of La Befana may even stretch back to pagan times, first appearing in ancient Roman winter festivals as an aging Mother Nature delivering her last gifts.

The best place to meet La Befana in person is at lively Piazza Navona in Rome. The Piazza's Christmas Market, known locally as the Befana Market, bustles until January 6th, Epiphany, or l'Epifania.

Piazza Navona is dotted with fountains, shoppers, and Christmas cheer.

NATIVITY SCENES

Months of preparation go into the many lovingly constructed Nativity scenes, or crèches, that pop up all over Rome and Italy at Christmastime.

Beginning in early December, through Epiphany, you'll find them everywhere: nine out of ten Roman churches set up a Nativity scene, and all over town, signs direct visitors to a *presepio*—that's "manger" in Italian.

They ornament piazzas, porticos, and even train stations. There's an annual exhibition of 100 *presepi*, made by artists and schoolchildren, at Rome's Piazza del Popolo. The mangers vary greatly. Some are intricate and beautiful; others are of dubi-

Nativity figures are lovingly and meticulously crafted by Italian artisans.

ous artistic quality. Some are old and others are avant-garde. Whether they're tiny enough to fit in a chestnut shell or big enough for St. Peter's Square, each one is unique, a window into the imagination of its creator.

In Italy, manger settings look like Mona Lisa's backyard, populated with animals and people you'd expect to find in the Tuscan countryside. Seeing the miraculous birth in a familiar setting, the faithful could relate more easily to the story. In manger scenes all over the world, baby Jesus comes with the local flora, fauna, and even skin color . . . just like the baby next door.

Up until the 16th century, Nativities were found mostly in monasteries and churches. In the 17th century, noble Roman families started setting up grand manger scenes

Romans go nuts for offbeat manger scenes.

in their homes. Artists were commissioned to create the figures, and class-conscious families competed for the most beautiful scene, opening their houses to visitors. By the 19th century, terra-cotta figures could be mass-produced from molds, and manger scenes began showing up in the homes of more humble families.

Now every Italian family has a *presepio*. Some families add another figure to the scene each day of the season, but only on Christmas Day does the Birthday Boy make his appearance. My Roman friend Francesca stresses that it makes no difference whether a Nativity is elaborate or humble in its materials and construction. She says the important point is that the Nativity brings rich and poor together. Christmas Eve is a time when everyone meditates on the same story—the birth of an extraordinary child, born in the most ordinary circumstances.

The baby Jesus takes center-stage, but not until Christmas Day.

ST. FRANCIS AND THE FIRST MANGER SCENE

The first Nativity scene was staged on December 24th, 1223, in the simple monastery at Greccio by St. Francis of Assisi as a tool to teach the uneducated, yet faithful, the story of the first Christmas. He built a manger in a cave, then brought the scene to life using real animals and local people playing the roles of Mary, Joseph, shepherds, and kings. The "living Nativity" scene, popular all over Christendom ever since, is especially popular in Italy.

On Christmas Eve, the small hermitage of Greccio remembers St. Francis' first living Nativity by staging a recreation in the same cave used by the saint.

Living Nativities, first popularized by St. Francis of Assisi, bring the Christmas story to life.

On December 24, 1223, a group of barefoot monks led villagers to the hill town of Greccio. From there they wound their way up a mountain to a stone sanctuary that was little more than a few connected caves. In one of the caves a layer of straw had been spread on the earth floor and a feed box placed in a corner; also on display were a donkey and an ox, as well as a number of peasants who had been borrowed from a local feudal lord. Throughout the long night, a procession of villagers climbed up to the cave to see this unique tableau, their torches illuminating the dark hillside path.

In staging this living Nativity, St. Francis' intent was to remind people of the humble circumstances surrounding the birth of Jesus. He said he wanted "to portray the Child born in Bethlehem, to see the hardships a newborn babe must endure, how he was placed in a manger and how he lay in the straw between the ox and the ass."

Today's re-creation in the sanctuary in Greccio on Christmas Eve is a reminder of St. Francis' original celebration. It's a simple, moving ceremony, with a candlelight procession up the mountain to view the humble scene, just as those faithful villagers did eight centuries ago.

ROMAN CRIB CRAWL

If you're in Rome during Christmas, do as the Romans do and pop into local churches to check out the *presepi*.

For a bit of manger history, visit the Basilica of Santa Maria Maggiore. There you can see five wooden planks, which are said to be from the original manger itself.

One of the most important holy relics in Rome, especially at Christmas, can be found at the Church of Santa Maria in Aracoeli. The Santo Bambino, a statue of the holy child, is thought to have been carved from olive wood taken from the Garden of Gesthemene, the place where Jesus prayed the night before he was crucified.

The odd little figure is clothed in rich fabrics and covered with jewels. He's believed to have miraculous healing powers and is often stolen, perhaps to perform a miracle on demand. It's said that the Bambino's lips turn red if a prayer is about to be answered and pale if there is no hope. Children especially love the Bambino, writing him letters and reciting poems to him on Christmas Day. The figure of the Bambino is usually kept in a protective glass case in a chapel, but at the stroke of midnight on Christmas Eve he's presented to the church's eager and expectant congregation.

Santo Bambino may or may not answer your prayer.

LIGHTING THE CHRISTMAS TREE ON ST. PETER'S SQUARE

The Vatican's Nativity scene has always been *the* decoration on St. Peter's Square. It's quite large, and comes with huge chunks of fake sheep's cheese and bales of straw. But Pope John Paul II, who grew up in Poland and became the first non-Italian pope in a very long time, missed having a Christmas tree. So, early in his papacy, he added a Christmas tree to the celebrations on St. Peter's Square. And ever since, there's been a tree there along with the Nativity each Christmas (see photo on page 181).

For a Christmas you'll never forget, attend Midnight Mass at St. Peter's.

During our visit, thousands of visitors and pilgrims gathered around a 105-foot-tall fir tree, donated by a parish from Trento. The pope appeared from the window of his study overlooking St. Peter's Square. On this day, he thanked some Polish mountaineers who had brought trees from Poland to Rome to decorate his private apartments.

The pope lit a symbolic candle for peace. Then a children's choir sang *O Come All Ye Faithful* in Latin, and the lights flickered to life. The tree, said the pope, would remind "visitors and pilgrims of the birth of Christ, Light of the World."

"I am grateful for the trees you bring every year because they remind me of my dear mountains and my dear homeland," he said.

It seems that Christmas especially is a time when we all yearn for home.

Blessing children from all over the world.

PEACE ON EARTH

Each year the pope delivers a Christmas message. During our visit, a frail but determined Pope John Paul II called for peace among nations. He made an eloquent appeal for an end to violence, especially in the Holy Land, where Jesus was born. "Too much blood is still being shed on earth. Too much violence and too many conflicts."

After lighting a candle for peace in his window overlooking St. Peter's Square, the 84-year-old braved freezing temperatures in Rome to preside over Midnight Mass.

Thousands of pilgrims, worshippers, and visitors gathered in St. Peter's to celebrate Christmas with the beloved pontiff. Arriving in his pope-mobile, John Paul

Pope John Paul II celebrates his last Midnight Mass.

II, slumping from the effects of Parkinson's disease and severe arthritis, was greeted with emotional applause and joyful cries of "*Pappa! Pappa!*" as he made his way toward the altar. His frailty reminded us all of our mortality, as well as the eternal life symbolized by Christ. Not without effort, he beamed and waved and blessed the masses, perhaps knowing this would be his final Christmas on Earth.

FRUITCAKES, AND
OTHER ENDURING TRADITIONS

Italians love to eat, and Christmas is a season of only-once-a-year specialties. These can vary from region to region, but you'll find one constant—fruitcakes.

Friends gather in the piazza to toss the panforte *around. The idea is to actually throw this local fruitcake closest to the edge of the table without having it slide off.*

In Italy, fruit-"cake" is disguised as bread, or *pane*. There's big bread *(panettone)*, golden bread *(pandoro)*, strong bread *(panforte)* and sweet bread *(pandolce)*.

Panforte is a dense mixture of honey, candied fruit, nuts, and spices. It has many virtues, among them the fact that it's easy to make and keeps for weeks. (It's rugged enough to toss around at parties and still consume later!) Culinary historians debate its exact origin, but *panforte* might have been invented in the 12th-century bakeries of Sienese monks. Because of its durability, wives and mothers of medieval knights going on Crusades sent their boys off with *panforte* in their lunchboxes.

Every Italian region has its own seasonal specialties. Tuscans prefer the medieval *panforte*, Ligurians love their *pandolce*, and Neopolitans turn their noses up at anything

Italy's traditional Christmas fruitcake makes a good dessert, gift, or shuffleboard puck.

other than *struffoli*. Only *panettone* (Toni's bread), originally from Milan, appears all over Italy at Christmastime.

According to legend, *panettone* was invented by accident. Toni, the baker, had fallen for lovely Lucia, who came every morning from the country to sell him eggs. Toni decided to woo Lucia by baking a scrumptious cake for her. Only wanting the best, he combined the freshest eggs with the sweetest butter and jewel-like candied fruits. But poor Toni was nervous—love made his hand tremble when he added the yeast, and he poured in a whole pack. Fortunately, Cupid smiled and the *panettone*, light and rich, rose in the oven to golden perfection. And so it was that *panettone* was invented. Toni and Lucia got married, made lots of money, and their marriage proved to be as sweet and long lasting as fruitcake.

And we have a winner!

Panettone di Milano

Start this *panettone* early in the day.

⅓ cup plus ½ cup warm water (100°F to 110°F)
2 packages active dry yeast
4 cups all-purpose flour
⅔ cup sugar
6 large egg yolks
1½ sticks softened unsalted butter, plus additional softened butter
2 cups golden raisins
1 cup candied citron

To make the sponge, pour the ⅓ cup warm water into a bowl and sprinkle 1 packet of yeast over it. Let stand until the yeast has dissolved (about 10 minutes) and stir in ½ cup of flour. Cover and let stand 30 minutes.

Sprinkle the remaining packet of yeast over the remaining ½ cup water in another small bowl. Let stand until dissolved.

In a large bowl, beat together the sugar, egg yolks, and the yeast-and-water mixture. Stir in the sponge mixture. In the bowl of an electric mixer fitted with a paddle attachment, combine the 1½ sticks of butter and remaining 3½ cups flour. Continue beating and slowly add the egg mixture. Beat on high speed until dough is elastic-looking and smooth. Beat in raisins and citron. Transfer dough to an oiled bowl. Cover and leave in a warm place as it rises; allow two to three hours.

Divide into three loaves. Roll them into oblong shapes and place in bread pans lined with buttered, brown paper. Cover and let rise again, until doubled, for about 2 hours.

Preheat the oven to 375°F. Cut an X in the top of each loaf with a razor. Insert a dot of butter into the X and bake 10 minutes. Lower the heat to 350°F and bake for an additional 30-40 minutes. Loaves are done when a skewer inserted in the center comes out clean.

Panforte di Siena

(Serves 8 to 10, makes one 9-inch cake)

1 cup whole hazelnuts
1 cup natural shelled almonds
1 cup candied citron, finely sliced
1 cup candied orange, finely sliced
1 t. grated orange zest
½ cup all-purpose flour
2 T. unsweetened cocoa powder
1 t. ground cinnamon
¼ t. ground coriander
¼ t. ground cloves
¼ t. freshly grated nutmeg
Softened butter
⅔ cup honey
⅔ cup sugar
Confectioners' sugar

Heat the oven to 350°F. Toast the hazelnuts on a baking sheet until the skins blister and pop, about 10 to 15 minutes. Rub the skins from the hazelnuts with a kitchen towel. Toast the almonds on a baking sheet until lightly toasted, about 10 to 15 minutes. Chop the almonds and hazelnuts very coarsely. Turn the oven down to 300°F.

In a large bowl, combine the nuts, citron, orange, zest, flour, cocoa, and spices. Mix well.

Butter a 9-inch springform pan and line the bottom and sides of the pan with parchment. Butter the parchment paper thoroughly and set aside.

In a medium saucepan combine the honey and sugar. Bring to a boil, and boil without stirring for 2 minutes. Pour the mixture over the nut mixture and mix vigorously to combine. Quickly scrape the mixture into the prepared pan (it becomes stiff very fast) and pat the dough quickly into place with a spatula or dampened hands.

Bake 30 minutes. Cool until firm to the touch and remove the sides of the pan. Invert the cake, peel away the parchment and shower the cake with confectioners' sugar just before serving.

The ITALIAN CHRISTMAS TODAY

The Christmas season starts nine days before Christmas and lasts through Epiphany, on January 6th. For many families, Epiphany, not Christmas, is the big gift-giving day, when kids open presents delivered by the broom-riding witch, La Befana.

Flip-flopping the gift-giving tradition, the children deliver a Christmas treat—usually *panettone*—to older folks who don't have any family.

As in many places, Christmas in Rome is a time of giving. The spirit of charity is alive in the Trastevere neighborhood, which comes together to feed the needy and the homeless on Christmas Day. At the church of Santa Maria in Trastevere, the Comunita' di Sant' Egidio replaces pews with tables and the poor enjoy a feast pre-

Bringing a panettone *to a grateful neighbor.*

pared and served by the compassionate community. It's a joyful occasion and by all accounts, those doing the giving feel as blessed as those they feed.

Outside of Rome, in villages in regions such as Tuscany, Christmas celebrations are a little more rustic. The festivities, while low-key, are memorable. During a busy season that sometimes feels overwhelming, monastic and village life can be refreshingly simple.

At the 15th-century abbey of Monte Oliveto Maggiore, sacred music and prayer infuse the tranquil Tuscan landscape at Christmas—and throughout the year.

In small-town Italy, children post their letters to Babbo Natale, the Italian version of Santa Claus, in this special mailbox that mysteriously appears each Christmas.

Mailing a letter to Babbo Natale.

VIGILIA, A ROMAN CHRISTMAS EVE FEAST

During the day of Christmas Eve, pious people attend church and observe a fast, saving their appetite for the big Christmas Eve feast called the "vigil," featuring not a turkey or a roast goose, but . . . the Christmas eel!

Shopping for eels used to be a dress-up social event in Rome. The build-up traditionally began the evening of December 23rd. After hitting the Christmas parties, fashion-conscious Romans in evening gowns would stroll through the fish market (housed in the ruins of an ancient colonnade) in search of the centerpiece for their

Better than gingerbread! Romans pick up an eel or two for their Christmas feast.

Christmas feast. Today Romans no longer shop in ball gowns, but they still seek out deals on eels. The best ones are big, female, and ideally purchased alive.

On Christmas Eve, while the eel is cooking, Roman families gather around the home's Christmas focal point—not a tree but the *presepio*. They sing carols, tell stories, and exchange presents. They might draw boxes from the "Urn of Fate." Some boxes will be empty, some filled with goodies. They complete their *presepio* scene by placing the baby Jesus in his manger.

Then, like a typical Italian family, they sit down to a lengthy, multi-course meal. Starting things off is one of the meal's most important elements, the appetizers called *i fritti*—"fried things"—which include morsels of artichoke, broccoli, ricotta cheese, apple, cod, or lamb brain, all dipped in batter, then fried. Next comes the *primo piatto*, or "first" main dish, often spaghetti with tuna and tomato or clams. The vegetable dish is Roman broccoli—boiled and seasoned with olive oil and lemon, or sautéed with oil and garlic.

Then comes the main course—eel, called *il capitone*, served roasted or marinated. Top the meal off with a dessert of fruit and dried nuts, then bring on the classic climax, the fruitcake—*panettone! Buon appetito!*

SWITZERLAND

Fröhlichi Wienachtä!

WHILE SOME COUNTRIES have more rich history, magnificent manger scenes, and grand churches than others, the spirit of Christmas can be experienced anywhere in Europe. High in Switzerland, where the churches are small and villages huddle below towering peaks, the mighty Alps seem to shout the glory of God. Up here Christmas fills a winter wonderland with very good cheer.

A FAMILY CHRISTMAS
IN GIMMELWALD

My holiday stay in the small alpine village of Gimmelwald (pop. 100) showed me that old traditions can remain strong . . . and that staying warm is a priority. Ovens are

Christmas just isn't Christmas without the family. Rick is joined by his children, Andy and Jackie.

small, and because of this wood has to be small too, so there's a whole lotta choppin' goin' on. Many kids treasure their woolen stockings, handknit by village grannies such as Hanni Feuz, who lives in Gimmelwald's oldest house.

My friends Olle and Maria walk with me through the tiny town. "In Switzerland," Maria explains, "about half the people are Catholic, half Protestant. You can tell a village's religion by the size of the church and school. If the church dominates, the village is Catholic. If the school dominates, it's Protestant." We walk by a teeny church. "You see, in Gimmelwald, we are Protestant."

And being the land of Calvin, the most austere of Protestant Reformers, the Christmas decoration is understated. Wandering past the only house in Gimmelwald that has an abundance of colored lights, Olle points and says, "This is our Las Vegas."

In Switzerland, Advent windows are life-size and decorated with flair.

The decoration is humble but charming. Each home adorns a window for Advent.

While I grew up opening little paper windows on an Advent calendar—enjoying the building excitement as, day by day, Christmas approached—the Swiss village tradition is similar . . . but the windows here are real, with a different one opening each day until Christmas.

And the debut of a new Advent window often comes with an actual party. Under a cold sky—stars reflecting off the snow, the moon inside a halo—the village gathers. In a kind of roving block party, neighbors get out, meet friends, and enjoy grilled sausages, hot mulled wine, and folk music on the accordion.

On this night, all are happy that it actually feels like winter. (Lately, the ski season arrives late, often after the New Year, rather than in early December as in generations

This Advent window glows like stained glass.

past.) The hot mulled wine is ladled from a steaming cauldron over a fire—it serves as a magnet for the gang. Keeping hands warm and conversation flowing, the *glüh-wein* stokes the party under the brittle stars. Local sausages are held like big cigars, or wrapped in fresh bread. The accordion player plays only in short sets because he needs to thaw out his fingers periodically.

Heidi Cocoa

Hot Chocolate
Peppermint schnapps

Consume with view of mountains.

A warm mug of Heidi Cocoa puts a smile on everyone's face.

Men take logs the size of a four-foot chunk of telephone pole, cut the end into a point, and plant them upright in the snow. Coated with tar, they're set ablaze, torches to light and warm the cozy yet frigid occasion. In the distance, under flickering torchlight, children ride old-time wooden sleds, going up and down, up and down.

HIGH-ALTITUDE TREE HUNTING

Swiss children eagerly anticipate the day that Dad takes them into the forest to find and bring home the perfect Christmas tree. Olle, Maria, and their children invited my family to go along for the ride . . . the sleigh ride.

We gathered our gear—snowshoes, sleds, a snow bike, torches, and bags of local

wine, bread, and cheese for fondue—and set out, riding the gondola ski lift high above the village of Gimmelwald. The torches were a fun reminder that today, for this traditional mission, there was absolutely no rush. We'd be here until dark: playing in the snow, hunting and capturing just the right tree, and enjoying fondue in the hut of a friend.

At the top of the lift, I straddled the snow bike and looked it over: The front ski was connected to the handlebar and turned as a bike wheel would. It appeared to be a pretty fragile piece of woodwork, but I was assured that it was plenty strong for a top-heavy 200-pounder like me. From the top of the lift we took off: the children shrieking with glee on their old-time wooden sleds, me shooshing on my show bike—gingerly at first but gradually gaining in confidence—while Olle followed on the big sleigh that would soon be used to transport the perfect holiday tree.

Shake the tree to assess the quality of the branches.

Arriving at a rustic one-room hut, we stepped into a time-warp 1950s world. Stoking the stove, we pondered the photos of the village's seniors from days when they were young and full of mischief. I imagined herds of cows with their Heidis, enjoying the peace and serenity here before the age of ski resorts.

While some stayed to prepare the meal, those of us on the tree expedition lashed on snowshoes and set out dragging the empty sleigh. After a long walk, we began the search. Olle would give the trunk a good shake. As the snow cascaded off, the children debated the tree's merits. Even the smallest children seemed to know that it had to have well-spaced branches to safely accommodate the lit candles that would magically transform it on Christmas Eve.

Finally, all agreed that we had found our tree. It was cut, lashed to the sleigh, and we

Lighting the way with torches.

trudged triumphantly back to the cabin for our hot and tasty reward. The windows were sweating, the fondue was ready, and we gathered around the table for a meal that exemplified good living in the Alps.

FIGUGEGL

For the Swiss, fondue—a communal pot of melted cheese—is purely a winter specialty. Only tourists eat fondue in the summer. Fondue is served with a wonderful Swiss white wine called fendant. Local wine production is so small that very little is exported.

Olle explained what makes fondue so fun. "When we Swiss plan a cozy party we add

"If you drop your bread into the pot," Maria said, "you must kiss the person to your left."

Gimmelwald Fondue

You'll need several different types of Swiss cheeses, one pound total. Gruyere, Appenzeller, Tilsiter, and Emmentaler are all traditional choices for fondue.

Make the fondue immediately before you plan to consume it (it can't wait around) and accompany it with more Swiss white wine or black tea. (Serves 4–6)

1 clove garlic, cut in half

1 ⅔ cups dry white wine (preferably Swiss, such as Fendant)

1 cup (4 oz.) grated strong Gruyere

1 cup (4 oz.) grated strong Emmentaler

1 cup (4 oz.) grated Appenzeller

1 cup (4 oz.) grated Tilsiter

3 T. flour

3 T. Kirsch (cherry brandy)

1 t. lemon juice

Freshly grated nutmeg and black pepper to taste

2 loaves freshly baked rustic white bread (ideally from a Swiss bakery), cut into 1-inch cubes

Start by assembling your ingredients and setting them aside within easy reach: Mix the grated cheeses together in a large bowl (or large Ziplock bag). In a small cup, mix the flour, Kirsch, and lemon juice. Cut or tear the bread into small pieces and place in a basket or bowl, with the skewers nearby.

Rub a heavy-bottomed saucepan or fondue pot with the garlic, then discard the garlic. Pour in the wine and set the saucepan over medium-low heat on the stove (or place the fondue pot over the warmer). Stir and watch carefully to avoid scalding. When air bubbles rise to the surface, add the cheese in hand-fuls, stirring constantly, until the cheese is melted and the mixture is blended.

Continue stirring as you add the flour/Kirsch/lemon juice mixture. Season with nutmeg and black pepper.

Serve the fondue bubbling hot. Spear bread cubes with long-handled forks; dip and spin the cubes in the bubbling cheese. Sit to the right of someone you don't mind kissing. Enjoy a FIGUGEGL time!

'FIGUGEGL' to the invitation. (It's pronounced like a word: fee-GOO-geck-ul.) This stands for *'Fondu isch guet und git e gueti Lune'*—Fondue is good and gives a good mood. Read this and you know a good time is planned."

With bellies full and just a bit of a holiday buzz from the sprightly white fendant— my favorite Swiss wine—we lit our torches, snugged the tree to the big sleigh, and mounted the snow vehicle of our choice. As the moon rose over the Jungfrau, we zipped down the mountain and back into Gimmelwald.

SAMICHLAUS

Advent is all about anticipation. And for the kids, much of that anticipation is about presents—rewards not for being naughty . . . but nice. As we've seen throughout

Europe, every culture seems to have its own version of Santa Claus, who serves parents by providing children an incentive to be good. Here in the Alps, it's Samichlaus.

Each Christmas, Swiss children receive a visit from Samichlaus—that's Swiss German for St. Nicholas—and his black-clad henchman, Schmutzli.

Visits are traditionally on St. Nicholas Day, December 6th, but Switzerland's dynamic Christmas duo can arrive at any time. When Samichlaus knocks on the door, frightened but excited kids answer. Samichlaus consults his big book of sins—co-authored by village parents—and does some light-hearted moralizing. Schmutzli stands by as a menacing enforcer. Then Samichlaus asks the kids to earn a little forgiveness by reciting a poem. After the poems and assurances that the children will reform, Samichlaus allows them to reach deep into his bag for a smattering of tangerines, nuts, gingerbread, and other treats.

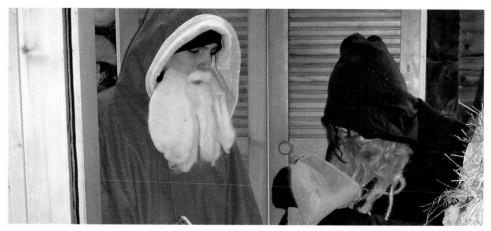

Samichlaus and Schmutzli go door to door in the Swiss village rewarding children for being nice. This year, Samichlaus was an American teenager (Andy Steves), and Schmutzli had an extra chore—translating.

CHRISTMAS EVE in THE ALPS

Traditionally, the family Christmas tree is cut and decorated on 24th. The whole family participates. Real candles, kept upright by dangling ornamental counter-balances, are attached, then lit by the children. The pine houses, with open beams, seem ready to go up in flames, but locals are confident with their candles. While the candles burn, presents are opened. The tree stays up until after Christmas, as candles are lit all over again on New Year's Eve—for good luck.

A classic Christmas dinner comes with boiled ham, cheesy scalloped potatoes, walnut cake, and finely decorated gingerbread cookies.

Lighting the tree with real candles—children's delight, fire marshal's nightmare.

If the family is religious, they'll often have a Bible that has been in the family for generations. The Swiss and German equivalent of the St. James edition is their Martin Luther edition.

Tonight in Switzerland, the grandfather completes the celebration by reading the Gospel story, the timeless tale that has brought together so many cultures for so many centuries: "And while they were there, she brought forth her firstborn son, and wrapped him in swaddling clothes, and laid him in a manger, because there was no room in the inn . . . And suddenly there was a multitude of angels proclaiming: 'Glory to God in the highest, and on Earth peace and goodwill to all people.'"

"... and goodwill to all people."

MERRY CHRISTMAS!

CHRISTMAS EVE IS FINALLY HERE. AND RIGHT ABOUT NOW,
all over Europe, our friends are celebrating this long-anticipated night
in their own unique ways . . .

In England, a boy hangs up his stocking. It's time to set out a snack for Father Christmas, then snuggle up with Mum and dream of tomorrow . . .

In Norway, they're gathering around towering trees on town squares, joining hands as they circle the tree in song . . .

In the Burgundy region of France, the beef is done! People are staying up late, just sitting down to Le Reveillon de Noël. There's a toast and a song, then the feasting begins!...

In Germany, a shopper makes one last purchase at a Christmas market...

In Austria, a bell rings, and children enter the room to discover the tree beautifully decorated and surrounded by presents . . .

In Italy, a villager honors the shepherds who came in wonder to see the Christ child . . .

In a Swiss village, the grandfather reads the Bible while the family listens . . .

THE SERVICE ENDS, THE LAST DESSERT IS EATEN, AND PARENTS tuck tired tots into bed. For a few hours, the world sleeps in peace, until it's Christmas! Dawn breaks, church bells chime, and excited children spring from their beds. It's another Christmas Day, heralding the birth of Jesus. Across Europe, people are wishing their families, friends—and even strangers—the same thing:

"Merry Christmas!"

Happy Christmas!

Gledelig Jul!

Joyeux Noël!

Fröhliche Weihnachten!

Merry Christmas!

Fröhliche Weihnachten!

Buon Natale!

Fröhlichi Wienachtä!

Ho Ho Ho!

ABOUT THIS BOOK

THIS BOOK AND THE RICK STEVES' EUROPEAN CHRISTMAS SPECIAL

THIS BOOK IS the companion of the public television special *Rick Steves' European Christmas,* first aired across the U.S.A. for Christmas in 2005, which peeks at traditional and contemporary Christmas celebrations in seven countries: England, Norway, France, Germany, Austria, Italy, and Switzerland.

In December of 2004, I traveled to Europe to film the TV show. This book comes from the research my crew and I did beforehand to write the script, as well as from

Locals had as much fun watching us as we did filming them.

lessons we learned while filming. After studying books, collecting magazine articles, gleaning material from countless Web sites, and getting advice from lots of travelers, I combined it all with the notes we took in the field. I want to thank the many people whose expertise contributed to the show and to this book.

The photographs in this book are primarily still frames taken from the TV footage. As it was shot in high-definition format, any single frame can be turned into a crisp still. With 50 hours of footage and 30 frames per second . . . that's 5,400,000 stills to choose from! The men behind the cameras are true artists. Thanks to Peter Rummel and Karel Bauer (who shoot nearly all of the Rick Steves' travel shows) for their beautiful photography.

Rick Steves' crew (clockwise): Santa, producer Simon Griffith, cameraman Karel Bauer, audio recordist Todd Schmidt, and Rick.

While we've produced more than a hundred travel shows for public television, this show presented unique challenges. As the Christmas season is short and we couldn't be everywhere at the same time, we employed two crews. I traveled with my longtime producer, Simon Griffith, on one crew, while Simon's wife, Val Griffith, accompanied by *Rick Steves' Europe* editor Steve Cammarano, led the second crew. To film one of our normal travel shows, our crew consists of just three of us (me, Simon, and a cameraman), but to film the Christmas special we needed a fourth person per crew: Since music is a big part of Christmas, we traveled with audio recordists for the first time. Todd Schmidt and Tom Levy were there to capture each ringing bell, each concert, and the audio bursts of delight as kids opened their presents.

Producer and co-author Val Griffith's crew at the Vatican (left to right): cameraman Peter Rummel, Val, editor Steve Cammarano, and audio recordist Tom Levy.

With Simon and Val Griffith, I built the script before departure. Each crew spent 14 days filming in Europe. Flying home on December 26th with 50 hours of footage, we edited the show back in our studio, where the sounds of Christmas rang through the halls well into spring.

When filming, we wanted snow to add Christmas ambience, but global warming is a reality, and winter in Europe doesn't usually kick in until January these days. We found Norway warm and wet. Thankfully, the first winter storm hit Switzerland right on cue and we got that wonderland flocking of our dreams.

Jackie and Andy Steves.

Christmas is a time for families. When I've watched other Christmas specials, I've been saddened to see a host without his or her family. For me, this Christmas special just wouldn't have been right without my children, Andy and Jackie. They flew in from Seattle for three days in Switzerland—just long enough to brighten the show with their smiles . . . and get over the jet lag before flying home.

Over the next few months, our initial book manuscript was shaped and enhanced by the writing talents of Gene Openshaw. The book evolved like decorating a Christmas tree—thoughtfully placing ornaments one at a time in just the right place.

Filming Christmas in Europe has its challenges. Even with two film crews, we could only be in two places on Christmas Eve and Christmas Day: Salzburg and Rome. Fortunately, we connected with local families in other places willing to celebrate the holiday early for us—so their kids ended up with two Christmases!

Gene Openshaw.

The soundtrack of Christmas is music.

Another challenge was collecting a variety of quality musical performances. We arranged some concerts in advance, then were treated to some serendipitous street-corner serenades, many of which we captured on film and on our companion CD.

The TV show was produced for public television to be used as a fund-raising special. If you received this book in appreciation for supporting your public television station, I want to thank you again for recognizing the importance of non-commercial broadcasting in our communities. I believe a society without public television is like a Christmas without lights.

The light of Christmas burns eternal.

Avalon Travel
A member of the Perseus Books Group
1700 Fourth Street
Berkeley, CA 94710

ISBN-13: 978-1-61238-736-9

Library of Congress Cataloging-in-Publication Data
Steves, Rick, 1955-
  Rick Steves' European Christmas / by Rick Steves and
Val Griffith.
    p. cm.
ISBN 1-61238-736-5
1. Christmas—Europe. 2. Europe—Social life and
customs. 3. Europe—Description and travel.
I. Title: European Christmas. II. Title.
GT4987.42.S74 2005
394.2663'094—dc22

                              2005015280

Printed in China by RR Donnelley.
First printing September 2013.
Distributed to the book trade by Publishers Group
West, Berkeley, California.

Additional Material and Editing: Gene Openshaw

Recipe testing: Mary Ann Cameron, Glenn Eriksen,
Sheryl Harris, Michele Kono, Monique Lee,
Chris Luczyk, Debi Jo Michael, Robyn Stencil,
Keith Stickelmaier

Europe Through the Back Door Editor: Risa Laib
Avalon Travel Editors: Patrick Collins, Jamie Andrade
Cover & Interior Design: Gopa & Ted2, Inc.

Candy canes (page 164) © Photodisc / Veer.

"Santa's Family Tree" graphic (page 37):
David C. Hoerlein.

For information on ordering the *Rick Steves'
European Christmas* DVD, see www.ricksteves.com.
For the latest on Rick Steves' lectures, guidebooks,
tours, and public television series, contact:
Rick Steves' Europe Through the Back Door
Box 2009, Edmonds, WA 98020
tel: (425) 771-8303 | web: www.ricksteves.com
e-mail: rick@ricksteves.com